THERE ARE ALWAYS

BLUE SKIES

...OVER THE DARK CLOUDS

Second Edition

JOHN RAYMOND WEST

Kendall Hunt
publishing company
4050 Westmark Drive • P O Box 1840 • Dubuque IA 52004-1840

Dedicated to

Mama

CONTENTS

FOREWORD

From Shakespeare to West

> *[....] My story being done*
> *She gave me for my pain a world of sighs,*
> *She swore, in faith, 'twas strange, 'twas passing strange,*
> *'Twas pitiful, 'twas wondrous pitiful.*
>
> (Shakespeare, Oth. 1.3.159-62)

What English professor can resist a good story? Who does not revel in hearing of dangers passed and survived? And what reader can resist a happy ending after harrowing the bowels of hell?

In defending himself against having used witchcraft and magic to woo the lovely Desdemona, Othello describes in the above passage the power of a storyteller to lure an audience. Desdemona is moved to tears by his stories and adventures and rewards him with "a world of sighs" (Oth. 1.3.160) for his efforts. And yet, the listener must beguile the storyteller to utter his discourse. The relationship is symbiotic.

Such was the experience over ten years ago when I first met John West. In passing, he would share some of his life experiences. My questions elicited more details and then more stories. Suddenly the storyteller realized that he had unique experiences to share. Some of them could move a person to tears, others to laughter, and still others to inspiration. With a little more prodding, I encouraged him to share these stories in the English and Sociology classes that we team taught.

Having appreciated my parents' efforts to record their own stories for my siblings and me, I relentlessly reminded him that his own children needed to know these experiences and revelations. And in the process of collecting, recording, and kneading these quite unique and often tragic events, it became clear to both of us that the individual, specific experiences represented universals to which many could relate.

A good writer is one who can make a world of a town, a community of a neighborhood, an everyman of one man. Such a writer portrays characters whose individual experiences reflect universal human emotions and thoughts.

There Are Always Blue Skies does all of this. Though set in particular locations, at particular times, and following a particular man, the experiences and emotions transcend such barriers. Like Shakespeare's characters, also set in specific times and places, this voice speaks to humankind. Many of us have experienced embarrassment, tragic losses, growing pains, moments of maturation and realization, almost insurmountable barriers, and dumb luck. And, if fortunate, we also have learned, survived, and perhaps triumphed.

As Desdemona came "with greedy ear" (*Oth.* 1.3.150) to consume Othello's stories, so we readers approach this book with open ears, arms, and hearts and beguile this storyteller to speak on. For a voice must have ears upon which to fall.

Elizabeth A. Elchlepp
Professor of English,
Santiago Canyon College

PREFACE

There Are Always Blue Skies represents an appeal to positivity. For the last five or six decades, our society has seemed to be fraught with unparalleled hostility and negativity. This book retraces the pathways taken by an African-American male in American society—from birth to the later adult years. The journey has been neither completely smooth nor direct. But there has been a wondrous balance, which has made for the essential ingredients that make life what it is meant to be—the bitter and the sweet.

The journey that begins in Birmingham, Alabama, in the early thirties weaves its way through a poverty-stricken, but protected, early childhood, through an awkward and uncertain adolescence, through a too-early and tumultuous marriage, through twelve very beneficial years in the Marines (including two invasions in South and North Korea and later service in Kobe, Japan). The consequences of these experiences point to the human tendency to survive against all odds, and that, actually, out of the negatives often times come invaluable lessons in patience, tolerance and resiliency.

The purpose of this effort is two-fold: (1) to allow for others to benefit from these experiences so as not to have to start at square one. Obviously, what has transpired in the life of one person may not necessarily work for others. But some of the lessons learned on this trip have universal application. The older one becomes, the more apparent that universality becomes. The awkwardness of coming of age is not unique to any particular group. People of different races, ethnicities, social classes and genders are all susceptible to the uncertainties of where they are and where they should be. To be in a disenfranchised group such as race, however, introduces an added dimension beyond the norm with which to deal. The effort here is to assure any interested group that it is not alone. And (2) to share intimate information with my children, similar to what I wish I had received from my predecessors.

At the very least, the information contained in this book has both anthropological and sociological implications. As we look at American society longitudinally, it is significant to note the changes that have occurred over the past half-century. This is not to indicate that things are even near where they should be in an enlightened culture. But the movement is in the right direction. Many of the social dynamics of the 40's, 50's, and 60's are all but alien to the newer generations in my classes. But we are not out of the woods by a long shot, and what happened before is an indelible part of our history that students need to know to ensure that history does not repeat itself.

ACKNOWLEDGMENTS

This is a humble account of what has transpired in the coming-of-life of a very fortunate African-American male, boyhood to manhood, in tumultuous times in American society. The account was instigated at the urging of my children who were surprised and somewhat fascinated by some of the raunchier details of my travels through life and insisted that they be reduced to writing for future consideration (for evidence to be used against me?). In the process of recalling some of the smuttier and more obscene events, I discovered, with surprise and a modicum of satisfaction, that there had also been some positive points to declare as well. Thus the *Blue Skies* theme. Hardly anything is all bad. Sometimes the good does not manifest itself easily and we have to prod a bit to find it.

I want to thank my wife, Suzanne, for affording me the latitude to pursue this undertaking, latitude that has been the pattern throughout our thirty-seven years of marriage. I readily attribute any successes that I have enjoyed to this newfound freedom. There were innumerable times when I chose not to be disturbed, even when important family functions probably should have taken precedence over my preoccupation with a project that I hope will be worth the neglect.

My gratitude to the good folks at Kendall/Hunt Publishers who facilitated timely feedback and production to accommodate my timelines, and to my daughter, Semara, for her patience in bailing out this dinosaur with computer technology on too many occasions, and to Carlo, my son-in-law, who, being the talented photographer, spun his magic with the graphics in this work.

Thanks to my colleague, Elizabeth Elchlepp, for prodding me to undertake this project as we team-taught honors classes in Critical Thinking and Social Trends and Problems. Many of my experiences were revealed to the students that she thought my children would find interesting. I hope that my children will forgive me for being simply human. Too often, I surmise, children perceive parents only as being above reproach. This book will certainly dispel that myth for any child who imagined me to be so. Elizabeth nurtured this work from beginning to end with ideas that only an English professor could envision. This project would have been literally impossible without her input.

Thanks to my students who continue to invigorate, challenge, and instruct me, keeping me nearly current in an ever-changing culture. The exchange of divergent ideas enriches us all. I have promised myself to never forget that.

And lastly, my heartfelt thanks to Mama, who is the very essence of all that has brought me to this point. Her undying belief in my worth, beginning with her staunch defense of a scroonchie baby, outstripped my tendency towards self-destruction. Her influence continues to dominate my persona, values and worldviews. I am my Mama's son.

BIOGRAPHY

Dr. John Raymond West is Professor of Anthropology and Sociology at Santiago Canyon College in Orange, California and Saddleback College in Mission Viejo, California where he has taught for thirty-five and thirty years, respectively. After twelve years in the Marines, he took a discharge and began his higher education pursuits at Santa Ana College as a thirty-one-year-old freshman. He then took his bachelor's and master's degrees in anthropology at California State University at Fullerton in 1969 and 1970. He earned the Doctorate in Education at Nova Southeastern University in Fort Lauderdale, Florida in 1975. At Santa Ana College he has served as director, associate dean, and dean for thirteen years. At all of the colleges he has taught courses in Cultural Anthropology, Physical Anthropology, Sociology, Social Psychology, Marriage and the Family, and Social Trends and Problems.

The three philosophers who have made the greatest impression on the author are Dr. Maya Angelou, for her uncommon creativity and vast life experiences; Dr. Leo Buscaglia, for his lessons in patience and expressions of love; and Dr. Martin Luther King, Jr., for his amazing courage in the face of unbelievable adversity.

Dr. West was Nova Southeastern University's Cluster Coordinator in Orange County, California for fifteen years, from 1975 to 1990. He has also been a lecturer at California State University at Fullerton, California. He has been a member of The One Hundred Black Men of Orange County, working primarily with high school youth in need of mentoring, tutoring and scholarships. He was the founding president of the Orange County Sickle Cell Disease Research Foundation. He has resided in California for forty-seven years.

After thirty-five years of teaching, he was conferred the Faculty Excellence Award in 2003. He was Orange County Teacher of the Year in 2006.

1

The
Beginnings—
Birmingham

It was like seductive thunder, with silky-smooth overtones.
It was highly inspirational and comforting.
It was authoritative
It was convincing
It was gospel.
It was bogus.

It was the first devastating, major betrayal that I would endure over the next six or so decades. And it was the first of hundreds of times that, in spite of life's many disappointments, I would always be reminded: *"There are always blues skies."*

It was my pastor and Sunday school superintendent, who was easily the most meticulous and articulate man I'd known by the tender age of twelve. He was the man I would hope to emulate some day, not having had a father that could impress me so. But then he was involved in rumors of a very explicit, graphic sexual scandal with one of the "good sistahs" (not to be confused with nuns in the Catholic Church) from the congregation. I was crushed, not being able to separate the fallacies of man from those of the church, a condition that we, all denominations, must continue to grapple with in our contemporary society. From that point on, I would always look around at church attendees and wonder who was doing whom. The positive consequences of that painful experience would not emerge for many years later when I grew to learn that you get over it. You pick up the pieces and you move on. As the trial lawyers say, "You can't unring a bell." Perhaps only in well-seasoned adulthood may we learn what we can control and what we cannot. Ultimately, that is the essence of "intelligence."

The "Beginnings," for me, were mixed, because in my youthful innocence my environment seemed pretty normal and secure. That is as it should be for unsophisticated children who are incapable of processing and sorting out the ugly details of life. The reality, though, was that in that time and place, without my being fully aware of it, there was abundant treachery all around me, both inside and outside my community. In spite of being naturally ide-alistic and trusting, I stood to benefit immensely from this initial trauma. It provided a layer of doubt that would protect me for the better portion of my life, though my natural inclination was to keep the faith. Smoke and mirrors are always there. It is a matter of one's ability to deal with them.

My story unfolds on April 9, 1931, in Birmingham, Alabama when I was born to Mignonette West, arguably the diva of mothers. (See picture 1, page cp-1). I know, everyone has that to say about his or her own, but this is the real deal. At four foot nine and ninety-five pounds, Mama was a giant of a woman and feisty enough to compensate for any physical shortcomings. I suppose all things really are relative. She referred to me, as a one hundred fifty pound adult, as her "brute."

Mama suffered no fools. When I entered this world on my birthday at Hillman Hospital, I weighed in at a little over four pounds. I understand that one of the nurses had the audacity to refer to me derisively as a "scroonchie" baby. Mama didn't swallow that too easily and proceeded to dress the nurse down with a vengeance. The nurse probably should have picked on a bigger mama.

On a certain level, I suppose all children are cursed (or blessed) with a measure of innocence. Your perspectives have largely to do with how innocence has treated you. Ignorance is bliss only if it has not hurt you. I remember the sweet innocence of dreaming of a magical, idyllic future with all the trimmings, even though we were living in almost abject poverty. Parents have a way of shielding their young from the harsher realities of life. In fact, most of our childhood peers thought my family was a cut above. We always managed to look good, thanks, to a great extent, to Mama's skills as a seamstress and her resourcefulness. Actually, I did not appreciate just how bad off we were until I reached adulthood and, with a different worldview, the realities came more into focus. As will become clearer and clearer, I am a slow learner.

Our family lived in a number of unlivable houses in Birmingham. By family, I mean Mama, my sister Miriam, and me. Mama and my father, John Henry West, were divorced when I was eight years old. We never addressed them as "Mother" and "Father." They were always "Mama" and "Daddy." And my sister was never "Miriam," but, to this day, to me she is "Baby Sister," or affectionately "Bay-Suh." And in spite of the fact that she was two years my junior, she always introduced me as her "Baby Bludder." I suppose male-female maturation factors had already begun to set in. (See page 32).

2

SIXTH AVENUE
SOUTH

The last house that my mother, father, sister and I shared as an intact family was in the fourteen hundredth block of Sixth Avenue on the Southside. (Back in the day, those streets on the Southside were referred to as Avenues "A" through "F." Today a level of sophistication has evolved, and now they are numbered streets, whatever that means for sophistication.) The house itself, a duplex, was fairly decent, compared to what was to come. The neighborhood, however, was probably the most threatening and violent of any we would ever experience. A restaurant on the corner attracted adult gangs of heavy drinkers, who invariably ended up arguing and fighting every Friday and Saturday night. A number of killings, usually resulting from stabbings, were witnessed by neighborhood children, me included. That violence should have set the tone for my perspective on what is normal in life. On the contrary, it had just the opposite effect, establishing a profound adversity to conflict and contention for my remaining years. The violence was not restricted to the streets, though. This was the first time I witnessed my mother being physically and verbally abused by my father. He became extremely angry about something and physically struck her while shouting obscenities. However, thanks to her resolve, it would also be the last time she would tolerate his cowardly behavior, though there would be similar such occasions later at the hands of my stepfather.

These incidents also set the tone for my attitude regarding gender relationships for the rest of my life. I became a feminist long before it was fashionable to do so, believing in absolute social, economic, and political gender equity, and believing that no community can survive without the contributions of both genders. A major problem for most men is the stigma attached to feminism, which is often thought to be synonymous with homosexuality. For women, it is the problem of not being capable of discerning the contrast between "feminism" and "radical, bra-burning, man-hating feminism." I seriously question the character and self-esteem of any person, man or woman (and there are both) who has a problem with the notion of gender equity. I have pretty good reasons to have ambivalent feelings regarding this issue as a result of having my philosophy come back to bite me in the hind parts by the very people with whom I empathize. Sometimes it takes focus, patience, and enormous fortitude to keep the faith, realizing that even women, as a result of previous conditions of servitude, can often come full circle and become as vicious as their former oppressors. More about this later.

An Interlude

After the divorce, Mama, Bay-Suh and I spent about a year in Georgia. We first stayed with Mama's nurse friend from her college days, Ella Mae Anderson, and her physician husband, Dr. Harrison Anderson, as Mama taught dance and recreation in the Atlanta Parks system. Bay-Suh was kept by Ella Mae and accompanied her on her daily nursing visits. In the meantime, I was sent to the country in West Point, Georgia, to stay with Ella Mae's parents, ostensibly to "fatten me up" on country food. (See cp-1, #2). Actually, after a full year of eating everything in sight, I did not gain a pound. I was what I was meant to be. "Scroonchie." Of the more than seven decades of my life, the one year spent in West Point was, without peer, the most memorable. For the relatively poor people with whom I lived, the experience was as close to the pre-Industrial Revolution period in lifestyle as possible, somewhere between hunter-gathering and pastoral and horticultural existence. There was social hierarchy there, also. Many, though not all, in the white population were doing very well, thank you. On a recent visit there, I discovered that those conditions continue to exist today, although interpersonal relationships between the races have improved. At least on the surface. I have felt fortunate to actually witness what life in this country must have been like when things were most basic for poor people. Hardly a moment or event has escaped me. The subsistence strategy was, to me, a romantic ideal. I doubt if it was so to those who had to scratch a meager existence from the earth. The family that I was with produced all food that was not hunted or found wild. Fruits and vegetables were grown on the small farm, as were animals, which were the primary source of meat. There was something magical about returning to rabbit traps and finding cottontails that had made the tragic mistake of going into the box in pursuit of bait. Curiosity kills more than cats. Probably, a major source of my fascination with this lifestyle was the conflict-free existence in West Point, quite unlike my experiences, to date, back in the city.

I remember the thrill of riding in the back of rickety, horse-drawn wagons. In season, I watched the ritual of hogs and cows being slain and butchered. Because sugar cane was big in the area, the family produced its own syrup, keeping a filled wooden keg with a spigot on the back porch. The cows were routinely milked, the milk churned to produce the best creamery butter and buttermilk I have ever tasted. I have never lost my taste for fresh-from-the-cow milk, in spite of its being horrible for the pipes.

3

SEVENTH AVENUE NORTH

For a time after my parents divorced, and before Mama's remarriage, we lived in our second horrible two-room, double-tenant house at 1000 Seventh Avenue North (now razed). The house accommodated two families, occupying two rooms each and sharing a toilet on the back porch. In order to accommodate our survival, Mama, who had graduated from Spelman College in 1928, was a former teacher who now had to work as a domestic worker in the homes of whites who were almost as poor as we. I say former teacher because during that era and in that place a woman would not be allowed to be married, have children, and hold a teaching job. It was thought that a woman's responsibility should be confined exclusively to the home and her children, that the breadwinner role should be assigned exclusively to men, and that a woman could not possibly do both jobs effectively. This partially accounts for why there were so many "old maid" teachers in those years. Here I had my first exposure to Mama's anger at many things that I did not really understand. Her anger surfaced in reference to my estranged father and her unforgiving attitude towards racism. She was angry with my father because of his abuse towards her, and with racism because of the denigration she felt by being denied the opportunity to pursue her career as a teacher and being relegated to subservient roles. My father was definitely *persona non grata* on visits to our home, and, as a result of the prejudice and discrimination she suffered at the hands of whites, she had no use for them under any circumstances.

In the college classes that I teach in Cultural Anthropology and Sociology, I have, over the years, frequently brought up the subject of my childhood as an example of life chances based upon poverty, racism, and the overall consequences of social stratification. The picture that I usually paint of Birmingham, I slowly began to realize, was not an accurate depiction of the city I once knew as home. In the attempt to be fair to Birmingham, to students, and to myself, I felt the need to visit my hometown and get a better, although cursory, look at the city as it exists today. I was, of course, pleasantly surprised at the change in much of the human condition, but disappointed with the abandonment and disrepair in the areas that I had known as home in my childhood. Because I learn slowly, it has taken some time for me to realize that it is true that you "can't go home again." Practically all of the changes that had occurred were sorely needed, including the razing of four of the five houses we once occupied, three to make room for the sprawling University of Alabama, Birmingham. Ironic that a campus of the University, the door in which George Wallace had taken his infamous "Segregation Today, Segregation Tomorrow, and Segregation Forever!" stand in Montgomery, would now serve to assist in making for a somewhat more enlightened and sophisticated community. Many of the communities that had been supplanted really had not been fit for human consumption in the first place. There does seem to be a natural romantic tendency for us to want to return to familiar places and find them as we left them. Most often they are likely to look smaller and uglier than memory recalls. On a 2008 brief visit, I was depressed with further deterioration of many of the familiar neighborhoods. I was also amazed that many abandoned, dilapidated homes which were disintegrating, had not been ordered to be cleaned up and removed. I wondered how many of the former owners had simply walked away from them, leaving no trace of their whereabouts.

The houses were one thing. The nature of the population was quite another. The joblessness, homelessness, and the abundance of obvious ignorance among the poor were more pervasive and threatening than ever. I wondered where all of the wonderful homes that are depicted in my monthly *Birmingham* magazine were located. And, more importantly, who occupied them. It makes sense that the magazine has kind of a "Chamber of Commerce" tinge to it. It is slick, depicting Birmingham as the final word in class, in opportunity, and an acceptable level of diversity. As I toured the areas with which I was familiar, in the areas which represented the center of the city and where the less fortunate resided, I saw nothing but depression. Where are these wonderful communities advertised in the magazine? I'll bet they actually exist and that a few African-Americans reside there as well. I also noticed that the publication was mostly about wonderful gourmet foods (which one of the most obese areas in the country does not need), weddings and other social events, and fine houses, which are out of the reach both geographically and financially for many of the citizens with which I was familiar.

Because Mama could no longer ply her profession as a teacher, she was now reduced to working in the homes of white people who were less educated and less polished than she and who could ill-afford to hire someone to perform their domestic chores. They would use racial slurs, make derogatory remarks about Blacks, and show no regard for her presence in their sexual lives. In other words, she was treated as a "non-person." Very often at the end of the week there was little or no pay (which was already meager) or Mama would be paid in used goods, e.g., clothing, toys, etc. Mama would be depressed and angry, with no recourse. Bay-Suh and I did not understand the gravity of the situation and, in fact, felt no sense of deprivation. I will always remember receiving a used rubber Charlie McCarthy doll, with the paint chipped away. I absolutely cherished that doll. And while Mama was bitter, I could not understand why she did not appreciate our good fortune as we did. But then, as children, we couldn't appreciate her concern for providing food and shelter for the three of us, which couldn't be accomplished with a used Charlie McCarthy doll.

In addition to this depressing situation, Bay-Suh and I, at the ages of six and eight, were necessarily left at home alone while Mama worked. We were left with a very specific list of "do's" and "don'ts." "Don't open the door for anyone." "Don't open the door to go outside." "Don't open the door period." "Don't touch this." "Don't touch that." In other words, we were in lock-down, which, when viewed in the context of today's enlightenment, was a hazardous situation. But never mind hazardous. We always knew to follow Mama's instructions explicitly, and literally for years thereafter, my younger sister held me hostage with a list of my violations held over my head as leverage to keep my mouth shut about her few errant ways. My serious transgressions included, for example, drinking out of a forbidden cup, one that was a part of a set kept in a cabinet, or threatening to open the door to test the limits. Her use of the phrase "I'm gonna tell Mama" was more than sufficient to keep me in line.

One of the most profound ways that Mama manifested her anger was towards my estranged father, who had apparently done far more damage in their relationship than I could possibly have realized. He would always come around to pick Bay-Suh and me up for some weekend visitations and a tour among his friends "In high places." He was a social climber, which was disgusting to both Bay-Suh and me. He would use the occasion to ask us to intercede on his behalf by asking Mama to take him back. We could not understand why she was totally unreceptive. By this time she absolutely detested the man. It would be years before we would be able to figure it out. After all, it seems that most children, by far, are eager and hold out hope against hope that a fragmented family will sort things out and become intact again. In many cases, this hope is carried right into adulthood. The younger the children, the more resilient and the more secure they are likely to feel, regardless of grownups' problems. For with the younger ones, their whole worlds have not been totally decimated by their parents choosing to go their separate ways, which, on the other hand, is often the situation with older ones whose worlds have been turned upside down. It turned out that my father was abusive (which we had witnessed), an addicted gambler, and a philanderer (which, as children, we knew nothing about). But he was a hard and steady worker, having worked at Southern Railway from the age of 14 until they let him go at 51 with no retirement benefits. He died of lung cancer at the age of 59. He smoked himself to death. Two packs of unfiltered Chesterfields a day since the age of 14.

But Bay-Suh and I, in the earlier, naive years, always adored him, because he was never completely out of touch and because he sporadically provided us with fascinating things with which we were unfamiliar. Of course, we did not understand nor care that the goodies were only sporadic. Once, when I was fourteen, after he had won big money on a Joe Louis championship fight, he took me downtown to a nice men's store and let me choose three suits—a blue serge, a gray chalk stripe and a tweed. Then he bought me my first alto saxophone, a Selmer, which would pay dividends for me throughout my adolescent and adult life. Sporadic or not, what kid would not be impressed with that sort of "generosity?" He was what would be called a "Disneyland Dad" today. Some weekends. Though Mama showed absolute disgust when he failed to pick us up on weekends as promised, Bay-Suh and I were quite forgiving.

The problem was, though, that gambling has its peaks and valleys. Mostly valleys. I got my first look at how it works when my dad bought me my first, last, and only used bike in childhood. Based upon my obvious pride, one would have thought that it was the fanciest bike in the world. In reality, it was about as basic as it gets—a frame, handlebars, pedals and a chain. I was always having to repair the chain, and with oily and grimy fingers, got very good at it. The bike seemed to have been repainted a number of times, without benefit of sanding or any other preparation. It really didn't matter, for my dad came by one day to pick up the bike, ostensibly to get it "overhauled." I hadn't noticed that anything was wrong with it. I never saw that bike again. As a result, the pain and disappointment that I felt for years was excruciating. Even today, I have a difficult time with that loss. I wonder how a father could possibly do that to a child.

Daddy was uneducated, a meticulous dresser, and seemed to have the need to rub elbows with the "right" people, people who were apparently of higher economic status, e.g., proprietors of businesses—restaurants, funeral homes, insurance companies—and families with "Negro old money." By the standards of most affluent white people, this was not very much. It crushed me to witness him ingratiate himself to people for whom I, even as a child, had utter contempt. I will never forget a scene, as I accompanied him on his rounds paying his weekly bills, when he humiliated himself by "yas suhing" a young, barely post–adolescent, pimply-faced white postal clerk as he purchased money orders. I was totally embarrassed and wondered how a man who would physically abuse a woman could vilify himself by being seen in such a pitiful state in the presence of the virtual "boy" behind the counter. But, more importantly, I wondered how he could allow himself to be perceived that way in the presence of his impressionable son. At that moment, I vowed to never, ever allow myself to be subjugated to anyone in that manner. I hate the term "boss" and never use it, and I wonder about people who feel comfortable using it (although I am aware that many are simply playing the game or that the term has no negative connotations for them). It's a game that I simply can't play. I am quite aware that no matter who and where we are in the hierarchy, we must be responsible and answer to someone. It's the way things get done. But "boss?" I have always believed that things get done best when there is collaboration among all the players and that individuals simply have different roles, all sharing equal responsibility, credit, and blame. When something goes awry, you find out why and ensure that it does not reoccur. I am certain that my attitude has hurt me politically and professionally, but I sleep well at night and have no problem with what I see in the mirror each morning, except maybe a face that would stop a clock.

One other significant thing happened at that first address on Seventh Avenue North. Mama had a suitor. Mr. Napoleon. She was very discreet, and Bay-Suh and I never really got a handle on the relationship. We just knew that he was a family friend, who was likable, handsome, tall, and polished. By the way, Mr. Napoleon lived "On the Hill" to the north where some of the more affluent African-Americans lived, and where Mama had grown up and lived until she went off to college. We never knew what eventually happened with that episode. But I remember a very melancholy Mama listening to a record entitled, "I Get Along without You Very Well." As strong a woman alas she was, I did see her cry on several occasions, and it broke my heart. This was such an occasion. It sometimes saddens me to think of how much undeserved pain she must have felt in her life and that she felt the need to hide it. Moreover, I wish that she and I had talked more about her life, which would have been possible in my adult years if I'd had the foresight to press the issue. But we all know how hindsight works.

Bay-Suh and I always wondered why Mama had chosen to reject a rather middle- to upper-middle-class background and lifestyle "On the Hill" in favor of bad marriages and a lifestyle bathed in poverty. Was it rebellion against the high expectations her family of origin imposed on her? The expectations were justified, for Mama was a high achiever. When she graduated from

Spelman College with a teaching degree in 1928, she was only eighteen years old. Her choice of lifestyle would make for a pretty tough existence. Was that what she wanted? Did she see her existence to be disingenuous? Did I get my disgust with artificiality and phoniness from her? If so, I want to thank her, for it makes decision-making easier and clearer, and I appreciate not having to look over my shoulder and second-guess myself, a benefit which has emerged particularly at the latter stages of my life, probably when it mattered most. The *blue skies* regarding the aging process involves being imbued with massive levels of self-satisfaction—later. As we grow older, we tend to become more and more contented with what got us to where we are. However, sometimes that can be problematic as we become set in our ways and are incapable of moving to the next plateau.

Birmingham proper is situated, for the most part, in a valley, between two mountains. In my childhood, the southernmost "hill" was inhabited by mostly well-to-do whites. The "hill" to the north was partially occupied by the few Blacks who were doing fairly well economically. That is also where "Dynamite Hill" was located, the area where Civil Rights leaders, such as Reverend Shuttlesworth, had their homes repeatedly bombed during the movement that followed later. That is where Mama's family of origin had resided. That is what Mama chose to forsake. The remaining years of her life in Birmingham would be spent in the flatland.

4

THIRTEENTH STREET SOUTH

Our second house was at 222 South Thirteenth Street (now razed), which represented the very worse living conditions we would ever know, but the area now looks unbelievably decent as a light industry complex. It was another two-room (not bedrooms) double tenant dwelling in an unbelievable slum. In a recent discussion with my sister, she recounted how disappointed she was that we were moving from bad to worse. Where previously we had a shared toilet on the back porch, we now had four outdoor toilets shared by fifteen houses. One water spigot rising from the middle of the yard served all fifteen houses. After a good rain, human excrement from the toilets would float in the puddle surrounding the water spigot. We then had to put bricks in the puddle and a board on the bricks in order to get to the spigot. Heating the water would be done on a wood stove in one of the two rooms. Mama and our new stepfather shared one room, while Bay-Suh and I shared the other, which also contained the stove and the "kitchen" table. Our stepfather's parents occupied the adjoining tenement. I suspected that he moved us there to be surveilled by his parents, as he had been drafted into the Army for a short stint.

I was ten years old when we moved to the Thirteenth Street address. While we were there for only two years, a number of important incidents occurred which would largely impact what I would eventually become, which was not all good. It was the stage at which I would first be allowed to venture short and controlled distances from home. I was the family runner. I found myself doing errands that introduced me to vendors of all sorts—grocery stores, drug stores, dry cleaners, and such. With very explicit instructions, I learned to shop for Mama's needs, which included everything from bias tape to sanitary napkins. (I wasn't smart enough to be embarrassed.) "Sweet potatoes. Make sure they're baking size." Or "Fifteen cents worth of neck bones. Make sure he picks out pieces with meat on them." All of this had the potential for serious grounding in interacting with the outside world. But it also had the potential for serious drawbacks. Being a poor, uninitiated novice, I was ripe for all the temptations and hazards in my new world. And, of course, I succumbed.

On Thirteenth Street, I got the first indication that we were exposed to the arbitrariness of chance, as far as health care coverage was concerned. We had none. In fact, I didn't realize how at-risk we were until I thought about it in retrospect many years later. I went barefoot a lot and wound up with many scrapes, cuts, and scars on my feet from broken glass in my play environment. Most of the injuries, under normal circumstances, would have required medical attention. Medical attention for us meant a lot of

Mercurochrome and home remedies. Home remedies might include leaves, salves, spider webs, strips of shredded pillowcases for bandages, and other exotic concoctions, which sometimes actually worked. Never once in my childhood did I see a physician or a dentist, except for the one time when I spent several days in the hospital with pneumonia. I never heard the words "suture" or "antibiotic" until adulthood. Too often, poor people do not spend what is deemed to be non-discretionary monies on preventive or non-life-threatening healthcare. Discretionary monies were not at issue here. They were non-existent. When a family's primary concern is putting food on the table and keeping a roof over its head, if a member should go to a doctor, there had better be something wrong. And the last thing the family wants to hear upon returning is that nothing is wrong. Really, people who are hurting economically don't have the luxury of thinking of the benefits of preventive medicine, which is very closely related to life-saving early detection. And sometimes there is not the necessary knowledge base that recognizes that "an ounce of prevention is worth a pound of cure."

Many of my daily routines consisted of hazardous activities that required the safety net of health care. I still show scars from abrasions resulting from grabbing onto the rear of trucks while on skates, with or without the knowledge of the drivers. Obviously, this had nothing to do with intelligence, except maybe for the lack of it. Mama would have killed me to drive that point home, if she'd known what I was doing. There were also the ventures out to Munga (our term) to swim in polluted water that was runoff from Ingalls Ironwork's toilets (See photo cp-3, #6). We had to push aside the human waste as we thrashed about as if swimming. It is a miracle that we did not die of some terrible disease contracted at Munga. Maybe some did die as a long-term result. Blacks had no other options for swimming in Birmingham, except to commute to Ensley, some distance away. This may account for the fact that many Blacks in our community have not had the opportunity to develop aquatic skills, which are critical for survival since seventy percent of the world's surface is water. I still have not mastered swimming. How I got around that specific requirement for twelve years in the Marine Corps, I'll never know.

And then, there were times when my friends and I were run off from hermits' properties with threats of being blown to bits, often during rendezvousing in isolated areas at night. Other dangerous activities included spending too much time salvaging discarded potato chips and salted peanuts from the Golden Flakes warehouse and hanging around railway sidings to see what might be thrown out. Again, another place where we were continually threatened and run off. So, it appears that my family's physical and mental well-being was always in jeopardy, very much like the better than forty-seven million people in this country today without health care coverage.

While it is typical for average families to do weekly grocery shopping based on accumulated needs, poor people may buy one item at a time, and then only when absolutely needed. And what difference does it make anyway when you have a runner? Being a runner can also be perilous. When dispatched to the neighborhood grocery store, I had a serious obstacle en route. A bunch of young boys, mostly about my age and a little older, always seemed to be waiting for me. There was one among them about my size and age who was urged by the others to beat me up. He seemed to know how to go about it, and there was no contest. With the applause and encouragement of his friends, he seemed to be really enjoying himself. Maybe the *blue skies* here was that I was picking up some pointers that would serve me well later, for I never took another beating from another child in all of childhood. Welcome to the mean streets. Another important incident (which no child should ever have to endure) occurred at the Thirteenth Street address and would help to govern the framework for my lifelong view of gender relations. It was common for my stepfather, Walter Mason, who worked at Ingalls Ironworks and who was a good and steady worker, to get paid on Fridays, and we would not see him until Mondays. He drank and caroused the entire weekend and often came home penniless and hung over. For years, I never slept on weekends. I would lie awake at night anticipating his return, knowing that whenever the moment arrived, there would be a terrible confrontation, often leading to a physical altercation. I was always concerned for Mama's safety and wanted to be there for her protection, runt that I was. On one occasion, in the midst of one of their fights, I was really frightened that she was going to be hurt and rushed to her defense. I still have the butcher knife scar on my left eyebrow that I received for my effort.

As a result of that traumatizing incident, along with many others that were yet to come, I have a real problem with any kind of conflict. I can't stand yelling and displays of anger, such as slamming doors or drawers in anger. I probably suffered a tremendous amount of psychological damage from these childhood images, which is the dark side. The positive consequence is that I refuse to incorporate that kind of response into my own persona, which I hope makes interacting with me a bit less stressful. At any rate, I developed a total lack of respect for my stepfather, but was sentenced to be with him for a half dozen additional years. Why my mother chose two such men as husbands I'll never understand. I always wondered if she saw this new arrangement to be a better alternative to working in the homes of disrespectful white people. She must have been in a quandary, because either choice was denigrating.

My stepfather was a hoodlum. And he had the scars from slashes on his face and neck to prove it. He was a strange mixture of cleanliness and order with a violent and devil-may-care attitude. He was athletic, having played sandlot baseball with the Say-Hey Kid, Willie Mays, in his early years, and had a lot of interest in sports in general. But he always seemed to be open for a fight. One afternoon he and Mama were sitting on the front porch on a swing chatting when a male passerby gave Mama the eye and then made the mistake of saying "hello." Walter rushed into the kitchen, grabbed a butcher knife, and sprang from the porch, chasing the man down the street. I was horrified. Here's another killing to be witnessed by a child, I thought. I was very relieved that he didn't catch the man. Another incident involved Walter having gotten word that some neighborhood tough had said something disrespectful to Bay-Suh. He scoured the entire neighborhood looking for the boy. Again, it was good that he was unsuccessful, for there would have been hell to pay. I think he saw himself as a good provider and protector. He was a far better protector than provider. And there was the tendency to appreciate what was perceived as protection, for after all, he was usually taking on the "bad guys." But, upon reflection, one would have to wonder what the motivation was. Was it protection or possession? One night, after his excursions in the streets, he was entering the front door of our home when a shot rang out and he fell to the floor. Apparently there had been an incident in the mean streets, and two men in a car had followed him home and shot him in the jaw. All indications were that they meant to do more serious damage. For a long time he smoked with a cigarette holder. His jaw was wired shut, and it was thought by the doctors that to remove the bullet might cost him his life. It was very visible as a lump underneath his skin. So, he took it to the grave with him and, when alive, wore it as a badge of virility.

Thirteenth Street was the birthplace of my first venture into what could have led to serious deviance. It started with my siphoning off the cream in homogenized milk on the way home from the grocery store, then having to concoct a cock-and-bull story about why the bottle was not full. But it got worse. I was sent to the local supermarket, an A&P warehouse and supermarket, (See cp-4, #8) to purchase one large bar of Ivory Soap. This was after taking the requisite afternoon bath and donning blue short pants and a white tee shirt (Ivory soap colors). Being very clever, and broke, I figured that it didn't make much sense to pay ten cents for a large bar of Ivory soap, when I could steal the soap and pocket the money for better use. Candy, for instance. And so, I started through the checkout line, pocket bulging, only to be stopped by the cashier, who asked, "What you got in your pocket, Boy?" "Nothing," I replied. But it didn't work. The store actually called the police "to arrest" me. I was placed in a patrol car and driven home where Mama was sitting on the front-porch swing. Being small in stature, I was barely visible sitting in the back seat of the car. The very sight of Mama was at once reassuring and threatening, for I knew there'd be some serious explaining to do. As in all crisis situations, she was frighteningly cool. The policeman let me out and told her to take care of the situation. She did.

This was my first taste of seriously delinquent behavior. I was frightened out of my wits, and, had I been bright, this experience would have been a deterrent to future deviant acts. But, as I mentioned earlier, I am a slow learner. Our new digs were within walking distance of downtown and all of its magical department and five-and-ten-cents stores. First, there was Sears, Roebuck and Company, the first store we would encounter heading to the heart of downtown. Then there were the five-and-dime stores: Newberry's, Woolworth's, Kress's, and Grants. At Sears, we could purchase five or ten cents worth of shortbread cookies, or, in spite of clerks' protests, we could sneak the use of the foot x-ray machine in the shoe department. These were contraptions that were commonly used to fit feet to shoes in more uninformed times. I can't count the number of times we were shooed off from the machines by shoe clerks. Newberry's and Kress's (See cp-5, #9), offered the broadest array of small toys, including the little rubber cars that fascinated me so. Maybe too much so.

Typically, I was on a mission to purchase sewing materials, facial crèmes, deodorant, and such for Mama. On one occasion, having no money of my own, I decided to take two little cars without paying for them. I think that's called stealing. Not being the most skillful or sophisticated thief, I was once again detected and held in a storage room until the store detective arrived. This took some time, and I am certain that the idea was to allow me to stew in agony long enough for my miserable predicament to soak in. I was eventually set free, a crushed child with a horrible secret that would dog me for years to come. I had, at this point, plenty of time to consider what the repercussions might have been or might be if I continued down this path in the future. As I grew older, I cringed to imagine what could have been my fate over my lifetime. This wake-up call represents the inevitable *blue skies* beyond the dark clouds. *There are always blue skies.* If you survive the dark clouds.

The houses on Thirteenth Street were situated on three-foot brick pillars. My fascination with toy cars had to do with the road and bridge construction that I did underneath the house. Most of my toys were legally procured. There were tractors, trucks, derricks and all other manner of road building equipment. I suppose there were some developmental skills that came out of my engineering activities. Probably, though, the primary benefit was the alone time that allowed me to reflect and to be somewhat creative. It was also a good way to keep me tethered to home, which turned out to have both positive and negative consequences for me. Being kept close to home was necessary because at no point had I been allowed to wander about, as many of my peers did. I really had no street smarts, and, as a result of being inordinately sheltered, there was little chance that I could survive without gaining skills already possessed by my "peers." But for now, I was at a complete disadvantage in my environment, which seemed to be filled with children wise beyond their years. I was the odd person out. That self-concept worked against me throughout my adolescence. It would have been really comforting back then to know that low self-concept is typical of adolescents in general, and male adolescents in particular.

Another significant incident occurred underneath the house on Thirteenth Street. It was my first awkward exposure to male-female interaction. It was the first time I was made aware of meaningful gender and sexual differences and how uneasy the concepts made me feel. It all happened one day totally out of the blue as I was about the business of building my roads and bridges in the sand. There was a little girl about my age who lived in the house next door. It so happened that she was playing underneath her house at the same time. Our eyes met and we began to make little people's talk. Eventually, the banter got around to challenges, on which little people tend to thrive. My little friend finally threw down the gauntlet and promised, "I'll show you mine if you'll show me yours." I was caught completely off guard and, honestly, wasn't exactly sure of her intentions. It finally sank in that this was about exposing ourselves to each other, which left me non-pulsed, uneasy, and uncertain as to how I should react. I successfully negotiated for her to go first, and from a distance of about twenty-five feet we got a good look at undeveloped private parts. I always wondered what we accomplished as a result. In fact, I was a little sick at the stomach afterwards and haunted with tinges of guilt. It was here that I was first convinced that girls are far more aggressive about such matters than their male counterparts. Perhaps this is the result of a difference in maturity. Is there some correlation between maturity and deviance? The difference in maturity levels of males and females in all age sets continues to fascinate me, even today as I observe grown-up interaction. And, of course, the overriding question is "Why the difference?"

5

RAYMOND, THE WOULD-BE VETERINARIAN

I have always loved animals, and in a rather classic fashion, they seemed attracted to me as well. In my limited travels around the neighborhood, I often managed to connect with a stray dog that I would tow home with a rope around its neck, pleading with Mama to allow me to keep it. "He won't eat much" was my usual promise. They all wound up with the same name: Pup-Pup. They would stick around with me until they felt the need to move on, maybe because of the lack of available food. They were all mongrels, of course. In fact, I had never seen a purebred dog until my sister and I visited a rather affluent aunt whose family owned a couple of businesses and could provide their two children with whatever their hearts desired. Their economic status was light-years beyond ours. They traveled to California at will and planned to buy a chicken farm there for my cousin, Harrison, in a few years when he was of age. Among their trappings was a beautiful cocker spaniel with a long, glistening, black coat that shimmered with every move. It had a cute stubby tail that moved like a metronome when it was excited. I was totally fascinated with it all and could not understand why my mutt could not have such a tail.

Pup-Pup was in trouble, for one of my key aspirations in life was to become a veterinarian, in spite of my distaste and ineptness regarding anything that even *sounded* like "the sciences." And if veterinarians could do it, so could I. I sneaked a butcher knife from the kitchen, collected Pup-Pup, and headed for a wooded area where serious surgery was to take place. I found a nice spot with a large rock that seemed perfect for the occasion. Pup-Pup loved and trusted me, and as I felt along his tail to find a joint, he was, for the moment, relaxed and comfortable. With the precision of a skilled surgeon, I quickly and mercifully cropped "Pup-Pup's" tail, cleaned it up with kerosene, and wrapped it with a strip of clean pillowcase that I'd managed to spirit out of the house. The operation was successful and everyone was happy, including Pup-Pup with his newly acquired stylish stubby tail. Mama, of course never knew about this incident.

My love for animals did not stop at dogs. We lived within walking distance of the Sears store that I mentioned before. I had acquired a number of goldfish on different occasions for five or ten cents. Funny, but they never seemed to live very long. I now think that it was because I felt that the more I fed them and the fatter they got, the healthier they would be. In other words, I killed them all with love, tenderness, and food.

But goldfish were not the only creatures for sale for five or ten cents at Sears. When I could save up enough pennies from scavenging scrap iron and collecting soda bottles, in addition to the toy rubber cars that I would buy (and sometimes acquire illegally), I would purchase baby chicks for ten cents each, one at a time. There is hardly anything cuter than a furry little chick that is little more than a ball of yellow hair standing on two weak legs. After five trips to Sears, I had accumulated five chicks, which I transported home in little white goldfish cartons. I fed them with corn mash that I had managed to purchase with saved coins. I spent much time with them in my work area underneath the house. They became pets and followed me wherever I went. When I went to the little shop on the corner, they would follow me and patiently wait for me to come out. Then they would follow me home. We ran into problems as they began to develop and the yellow fur turned to white feathers, first on the wings then over the entire body. My pragmatic stepfather decided that it was time for them to serve a more practical purpose. I was devastated at the thought of their being used for food and could not be involved in any way with the meals they eventually became. Somehow, it seemed cannibalistic. They were my friends.

If the challenge by the little girl next door gave me problems with male-female interaction, it was the first of many negative gender questions for me. At this point, I had not yet been "smitten" and could not imagine the years of heartache and disappointment that lay ahead. I would now fall "in love" for the first time, if it is possible to do so as a nine-or ten year-old. Her name was May Katherine Hale and she was a knockout. It was obviously her beauty that I was in love with. After all, what else would I know about relationships and personal qualities at this stage of the game? It really didn't matter that much anyway, because my worldly and streetwise best friend, Joe McDaniels, wanted her and knew how to get her. She reciprocated, and, in wonderment, I found myself on the outside looking in. Joe knew what was really supposed to happen when playing the game of "hide and seek." I didn't. Joe knew how to French kiss and how to express declarations of love. I didn't. I wasn't far enough removed from my ten-cent rubber cars to think too seriously about methodology. So, Joe got the girl. I doubt that May Katherine ever knew of my feelings for her.

The A&P warehouse and supermarket was within striking distance of our house, and I spent major amounts of time foraging from among the box-cars that delivered goods to the store. I would collect perfectly good wood, dunnage for securing cargo, and use it for building a coal bin or a chicken coop or as fuel in the small fireplace or the wood stove. I would dig through the crushed ice that was used for refrigerating produce, sometimes coming up with real treasure such as ice-cold apples or carrots or oranges that had escaped from their crates. I'm pretty sure that Mama was not aware that I was hanging out around railway sidings, which was extremely dangerous for even the workers who knew what they were doing. (See cp-4, #8).

Our time on Thirteenth Street set the tone, to a great extent, for what I am today. It was the foundation for a personality derived from innocence, naiveté, and generosity to a fault. Generosity is the one characteristic for which I make no apologies. Leo Buscaglia once said, "The only reason for having anything is to share with others." At the blink of an eye, I would give my cherished toys away to children who had none, but who were probably no worse off than I. I think that subconsciously I was attempting to make them like me. I felt the need for friends. This may seem like a fine quality today, but at the time my folks, especially my stepfather, would be livid with me and lecture me on the rules as they applied to the real world. As it turns out, he was partially right. It was the way things were done then. However, he could not have factored in my innate characteristics and, therefore, what worked for me. It is true that at times I have felt gullible and easily duped, and I don't intend to applaud myself for being "so kind," for my tendencies could just as easily have been perceived as character flaws since the tendency was, and is, totally involuntary. The key for me has been to not be concerned about things necessarily being equitable. I always feel that when the dust settles, I will land on my feet. There would be plenty of times when I would need to hold on tenaciously to that thought.

Thirteenth Street was also my first direct encounter with racism. It had obviously impacted my life at every turn, but I was not aware of its dynamics. If it had had blatant effect on my rubber cars or my baby chicks or my mutt, I would have felt and understood its sting. My child's worldview did not extend beyond the things that mattered to me in my immediate world, such as in Jean Piaget's first stage of cognitive development.

The used bike that my father had bought me often took me on excursions beyond the limits set by Mama. One such excursion took me to the vicinity of Hillman Hospital, which has since been swallowed up by the sprawling University of Alabama, Birmingham. It is still there, though tentatively. I was not allowed to go into the streets with this full-sized bike, which I could hardly control. As I was pedaling unsteadily down the sidewalk, I found myself face-to-face with a white couple. Somehow, I managed to steer off the sidewalk onto the grass parkway, barely avoiding a collision with the couple. Though successfully executed, the maneuver was apparently not good enough to satisfy the man. Suddenly, after I had passed them, I felt a large hand grasp the back of my tee shirt, stopping me cold in my tracks. I will never forget the hateful, reddened look on his face as he pointed what I eventually learned to be a .45 automatic pistol (I would later carry one in the Marine Corps.) in my face and shouted, "Nigger, I will blow you from here to Kingdom Come!" As I read the anger in his flushed face, I was certain that he meant it and would have done it if not for the woman with him who grabbed his arm and pulled him away saying, "Honey, don't do it. He's not worth it." What a nice thing to say about a little kid in short pants who is absolutely no threat to anyone. I am now aware that when dealing with ignorance, it serves no purpose to attempt to get into the heads of people who do not know or care about the long-range effects of their actions. In this case, I am certain that the dehumanizing and denigrating effects were exactly what the man hoped for. Fortunately, it didn't work over the long haul.

Another set of incidents, which heightened my awareness of racism and insensitivity, came rather routinely at the hands of younger whites. It was customary for Mama to have my sister and me take early afternoon baths, don clean clothes, dust ourselves with talcum powder and accompany her on walks. On several occasions young white males who were joy riding, sometimes in convertibles, would expose themselves to Mama, a woman with her two young children. This was another source of Mama's anger. Many people in our society criticize Blacks for being too reactionary, too radical. I often wonder why, given all that they've endured, they are not angrier than they are. Heaven knows there is ample cause.

Michelle Obama's statement in the presidential primary that she was proud of her country "for the first time during my adult life" should be viewed critically and objectively. Anyone choosing to criticize her position should first consider the history of African Americans in this country. There really has not been very much to be proud about from their perspective. Even my own misplaced devotion, patriotism and indoctrination from childhood and twelve years in the Marines eventually became dubious as I took a closer, more sophisticated look at our experience on these shores. It simply has not been pretty. So, Ms. Obama makes a good point, one that cannot be understood by anyone who has not shared that experience. It is pretty easy, for those who have had unlimited opportunities, to make judgements based upon their own situations. In spite of her achievements, she understands what the masses in the Black community must endure, for in today's society, the lines between social classes among Blacks are very blurry, and, perhaps for the first time in our history on this continent, we understand that. We're all in the same boat, from the White perspective. So, this country seems to be embarking on a more positive course with regards to African-Americans in politics, something that we might feel good about. Why not say it out loud and hope that we may guard against regression and that we may witness progress in other areas as well, i.e., business, education, and employment. Of course, many would prefer for Ms. Obama to smile and say that she likes what's been happening to us. Fortunately, that is not likely to happen, thank goodness.

Bay-Suh and I attended Cameron Elementary School, another landmark of our childhood razed to make way for the University of Alabama campus. Cameron was memorable to me for two important reasons. One, the wood frame building actually leaned to one side like the Leaning Tower of Pisa, without benefit of being recognized as one of The Seven Wonders of the World. And it was definitely not a tourist attraction. On the contrary, though typical of many African-American schools in Birmingham (except for Lincoln on the north side and Washington in Titusville), Cameron School should have been the shame of any school district official at the time. We always wondered if one day when we reported to school it would have simply decided, out of sheer exhaustion, to give up, call it a day, and recline on its side. Its closest competition for the "Most Shameful" was Lane Elementary, a short distance away. It is noteworthy that these dilapidated buildings produced some wonderful students and lifelong lessons. This is, however, not justification for allowing schools to fall into disrepair due to years of neglect, with the mistaken idea that the pupils will be better off for the experience. It is always questionable if putting anyone through negative experiences is likely to result in positive outcomes.

Most importantly, though, Cameron was also memorable to me because it was my introduction to what I have always believed to be the most influential of all the teachers I have ever had—at any level—and there have been some good ones. Her name was Mrs. Lucille Boyd. The quintessential professional, Mrs. Boyd probably had greater positive influence on more people's lives than anyone I have known in the profession. She was a taskmaster who did it with love and consistency. Her teaching went far beyond things academic. Many children came from homes that, to say the least, did not emphasize personal hygiene and decorum. They would show up with dirty body parts, and she would shepherd them into the cloakroom where she had waiting a wash pan filled with warm water. She would then proceed to scrub dirty necks, ears, and hands and suggest to them that they tell their mothers what she had done. (I suppose mothers had some learning to do, too.) I was fortunate. I never had to face the scrub brush, for Mama would not allow us to leave home dirty.

Mrs. Boyd also kept a supply of clean used clothing on hand to replace dirty ones worn to school. As she was having them change into the clean, sometimes tattered ones, she would remind us all of something that I will always keep fresh in mind: "You may be poor. You may have to wear patches on your clothes. But there's never an excuse for being dirty."

Another dimension of our education with Mrs. Boyd, beyond academics, extended to instruction in decorum and morals. Each morning, before anything else, there was a segment called "Devotion." Here, we recited Bible verses and sang religious songs, especially spirituals. Talented children with beautiful voices got to show their wares. Of course, all of this was years before such activities as religion in schools were at issue. As a result of these activities, I have always felt that there were benefits to be accrued towards our development. An important consideration, though, is that we were pretty much a homogeneous community. And so, the matter of religious differences was close to a non-issue. We were mostly Protestant, mainly Baptist with a smaller percentage of Methodists. There was room for a smattering of Catholics. After all, there was Immaculata High School (now called Our Lady of Fatima) in Titusville which was attended by African American children taught by White nuns. This was, in part, what made for consternation on the part of the White citizens, with their Jim Crow laws. The diversity in our religious denominations today and the greater tendency for one religion to impose its will on the others is what drives the need for objectivity in the classroom. More caution needs to be exercised, now that religion is such a prominent player in the political landscape. No religion, or non-religion, should be left behind.

As a direct result of my family's living on the wrong side of poverty's cusp, and our tendency to relocate frequently, Bay-Suh and I were required by Mama to attend the nearest church to our home, or whatever building with or without a spire was on the corner. We were required to go and to go often. Sunday School, Vesper, choir practice, regular church services, or whenever the doors swung open. Some would think that this would cause a lot of confusion, and I think that is a possibility. (It can certainly cause burnout, which I experienced very early.) We attended Baptist, Methodist, Presbyterian and non-denominational churches. Rather than being confused, I learned an invaluable lesson in religious tolerance. It is a lesson that most do not get the opportunity to experience because they are not forced to get out of their boxes, therefore, sticking closely to family tradition, which is likely to be provincial. While tradition may often work, it does not always do so. The tolerance that I learned could only be acquired through personal experience and is not likely to happen if we are stuck in the "holier-than-thou" syndrome. I came to understand that all the denominations have something good about them, and that they are all headed, generally, in the same direction. The problem is that provincialism often says to people that there is only one way, and that way is our way. This usually causes more conflict than tolerance. When we consider that most wars in world history have been fought over religion, it should give us pause. Groups often insist that all others become like themselves or not exist at all. Condoleezza Rice's grandfather pastored at our Westminster Presbyterian Church. (See cp-6, #11). I've often wondered where she went wrong politically (my perception). She is obviously an exceptionally bright woman. Sometimes Presbyterians saw themselves to be higher in the religious hierarchy than the others, but then relate themselves to the downtrodden when it becomes convenient or politically expedient. History will be her final judge.

6

TITUSVILLE

Perhaps at the urging of Mama's older and more socially connected sister, Aunt Mary McKinney, we moved once again. This time we would be moving to a neighborhood closer to the well-to-do McKinneys, though certainly not to a neighborhood on the same level as theirs. By comparison to our previous homes, we were now living "high on the hog," as the saying goes. The first measure of our new standard of living was the fourplex in which we shared an actual indoor bathroom with one other family. It was always kept spotless by both families. And it had wonderful linoleum on the floor. Three of the four occupants, including our family, were situated on the first floor, with a fourth renter upstairs. The upstairs people were always a mystery, for we never saw them coming or going. It is easy to imagine what

Bay-Suh and me, circa 1946.

goes on in the heads of young children who are prone to manufacture stories bound in intrigue. We just knew that the upstairs quarters were haunted.

Although much has been said about the significance of the first three residences that we occupied, this new one at 48 Fourth Avenue South was where the most significant transitions of my life occurred. And it was not all pretty. But there were many bright spots as well. We had absolutely wonderful neighbors, both within the fourplex and in the adjacent homes, all of which included boys who became close friends and grew up together. Fortunately for me, they were mostly as naïve and innocent as I. On one side of me was Harold Williams, a very quiet and handsome boy, who lived with his grandmother. His uncle, Ike Williams, was the music teacher for all of the children in the neighborhood, which accounted for Harold's involvement with the trumpet. Almost every child in our neighborhood played some kind of instrument. Even those who did not have drums played on pads hung over banisters until they acquired the real thing. (I think that parents were smart enough to prefer the pads to drums.) I wonder what has happened to music these days? Hardly anyone takes lessons in theory or piano or any instrument other than the guitar anymore. Once young people acquire skills to strum two or three chords, they feel accomplished. Has anyone noticed that there are hardly any school concert or marching bands anymore?

So important was my time spent at 48 Fourth Avenue that during a brief visit to Birmingham a few years ago, I parked on the street and strolled before the one remaining home that I had known so well and remembered so fondly. I stopped dead in my tracks in front of #48 when I noticed that the house number was an Ullman Junior High School woodshop product of mine from 1946 (cp-18, #42). Sixty years ago! (That workshop is currently the Forensic Anthropology Lab at UAB). Then and there I decided that it was mine and I had to have it. So, after my classes at Santiago Canyon College on a Thursday, I went directly to the airport, boarded a plane for Birmingham, rented a car, got a hotel room and drove to the home early the next morning before daylight. With a small crow-bar, which I'd procured at TrueValue Hardware in Mission Viejo, I proceeded to remove the old number and replace it with a finer tile and oak one that I had made. I always wondered what the occupants must have thought of their newfound good fortune. I did not bother to check with them first. The original 48 is now proudly displayed in my home. The rescue turned out to be a timely move, for during a recent information-gathering trip to Birmingham, I was disappointed to find that there was an empty lot where the house had stood. Fortuitous. (See photos 13 and 14 on page cp-7).

Harold's father lived in Buffalo, New York, and came home to visit his mother (Harold's grandmother) around the various holidays. He would bring his new wife along, with whom we young boys were intrigued. We were fascinated with her northern accent, which sounded so "proper." She was not only kind of pretty, but she also used phrases like "I fully agree with you," which was unlike any usage to which we were accustomed and which served to make her that much cuter. We had the same experience when Condoleezza Rice's father, John, came to town with his wife, who tended to impress us. Young boys are so impressionable (and silly), though I have learned that, to a lesser degree, so are girls.

The practice of grandparents, especially grandmothers, winding up with responsibility for grandchildren is not novel. It is difficult to know if the practice is more or less common today than in the past, but it has always been customary with the African-American community and I suspect with others. In the past, grandparents or other extended family would assume responsibility for the children, no questions asked, nor was there a big issue made of it. I can't imagine where many mothers and children would have been without extended family to step in and fill the gaps left by fragmented homes. It seemed routine for children to be handed over to "Big Mama" (the term for the father's mother) if only to free the parents to pursue the childfree lifestyle. Today, other issues are at play, such as young parents being addicted to drugs or being incarcerated, in addition to being simply irresponsible. Harold had simply been handed off to Mrs. Williams, who was as sweet as they come and who did a marvelous job of rearing him to adulthood.

On the other side of us in the fourplex were the Hopsons, with two nephews. Both were children of the woman's siblings. To the woman, Andrew Preswood was a sister's son, while Garfield Hopson was a brother's. Poor Andrew was worse off than I in that he was even more tightly tied to his aunt's apron strings than I was to Mama's. He was not allowed to spend time playing with the rest of us. He always seemed to have excessive chores or errands to do. The rest of us teased him mercilessly because we were aware that he had an "undescended testicle." But, of course, children being the cruelest and most venomous creatures on earth would never let him off with a nice term like that. We called him "One-nut Andrew." He was fool enough not only to tell us about it, but also to actually show us! It wasn't a pretty sight.

My real connections, though, were with what would turn out to be my lifelong best friend, William Garlington Downing. William lived in the house next to ours (which has also been demolished) with his grandparents and two older brothers, James (Scoop) and Alfonzo (Fonzi). Almost from the beginning we seemed to click; thus, began a series of adventures together that would only serve to strengthen our bond and make for the only best friend each person is promised and is likely to experience in a lifetime.

Practically all of the awkward things that can happen, as one transitions from childhood to adolescence, would now begin to happen. At the outset, my sphere of movement was pretty restricted to our block. The sheltering continued. I was not allowed to play pick-up basketball on the local school grounds. "Why, you might get hurt" was the familiar refrain. I was permitted to play stickball on the dirt road (later paved) in front of the house, under the watchful eye of grownups. All of us boys were still in short pants (when short pants meant "pre-teens"). I think that mothers are especially protective of "scroonchie" children and sometimes contribute to their stunted growth—both physical and social. However, in this case the physical part was hopeless, since I was the product of smurf-sized parents.

One consequence of the restrictions I lived with was my obsession with physical activities. For years, as an adult, I played basketball with the big guys. I could never get enough, even into middle-age when I finally wised up and realized that, for safety and health reasons, I would need to find a less physically threatening activity. I now play tennis two or three times each week. Tennis is a game for life.

Some of the most memorable experiences at the Fourth Avenue address happened as we, Bay-Suh and I, were enrolled for the next few years at Washington Elementary School, (which I was devastated to discover torn down on a 2008 visit to Birmingham) where our social lives began to blossom. It was the first time my name was tied romantically with a girl, although I had no part in the arrangement. Children have the need to size others up and decide who should be paired with whom. I was passively assigned to several girls over time. It didn't matter that there was no interaction between us. First, there was Georgia Turner, who lived on our dirt street where we played stickball. I felt obligated to sit with her in the double desk in our classroom and play my assigned role. A classmate, a bigger and stronger James "T" Johnson, sat behind us and continually needled me, making snide remarks and poking me in the back. The next thing I knew, the teacher and several classmates were pulling me off of him on the floor in the back of the room. I had lost all consciousness of what I was doing, until informed by the other kids. On only one other occasion in my life would I totally lose it, because rationality would usually intervene and I would consider the consequences.

Forethought is an excellent deterrent to negative reactions. The lesson to me was the positive outcome. I had taken my last beating back on Thirteenth Street and vowed never to take another one. *There are always blue skies*. This partially made up for all the beatings I had absorbed on Thirteenth Street. But not quite. There were other debts owed me.

Then it finally happened. The kids hooked me up with Lizzie Bea Hopson, cousin to Andrew and Garfield, my next-door neighbors. Because I was getting a little older and hormones were percolating, for the first time I was either interested or curious in the kids' pairing of me with a girl. But from the outset I got the feeling that Lizzie Bea was a little too fast for me, the novice. She wore the earmarks of a more mature person, one gold tooth in front, which was fashionable for older kids and adults in the day. She also wore grown-up bras, with intricate lace trimming, which she flaunted by leaving several top buttons on her blouse undone. Right away, I felt that I was in over my head. It was matchmaking gone awry. I never knew what became of Lizzie Bea or Georgia Turner. There were always saucy rumors when they disappeared from the scene, but the rumors were never substantiated in our circles. No matter. I was still more interested in games children play.

I was in for more pain as I learned additional facts about the difference in maturity levels of boys and girls. As in the two instances previously mentioned, it was not atypical for boys to get left in the dust as their female contemporaries outdistanced them in sophistication. Girls learn very early how to "work" boys. I remember young girls throwing down challenges to awe-struck boys with assertions like "I know I've got a good one, 'cause I can feel it when I walk." Their male chronological peers would wonder what they meant by a "good one" and how they ever got to be so confident and sure of themselves. And, unfortunately, the confusion and uncertainty usually happens at the most crucial time for males, when they are already grappling with self-identity. There is that tug-of-war between childhood and adulthood that is felt by both males and females. The expectation that males are in control, assertive, and decisive is a fallacy that sorely needs to be re-evaluated. Personally, I never had that problem, for no one ever expected me to be in control, assertive, or decisive. Actually, the converse was mostly true. I attempted to offset my deficiencies with bravado. This would continue until I began to develop a positive self-concept, which did not occur until well into adulthood.

If it is true that the first five years of life are the most crucial in a child's development, then certainly the next five are almost as critical, for the different stages are building blocks, and the foundation provided by previous years serves as potential for ensuing stages. Accordingly, I now see myself as an enigma, for although the chronological stages kept coming on schedule, I did not experience the progression that should have accompanied them. As I mentioned before, I was, and sometimes continue to be, a slow learner. Some call it retarded development.

My first kiss came as a complete shock, because it was a real kiss. I had been accustomed to innocent little kisses on the cheek and lips. But now came the awakening. William's cousins (all girls) came to visit on occasion from Cleveland, Ohio. Once again, we were fascinated by these cute girls who spoke "proper." I somehow got hooked up with what I thought was the cutest of them, June Gardner (June Baby). She was chronologically a bit older than I, which meant that in terms of maturity, she was aeons ahead of me. One evening, as we were all kind of "fooling around" at dusk, as kids do, she decided to plant one on me. I, in my shock, was wondering what the tongue was all about. And once again I knew that I was out of my league. The period was late World War II, and a number of young neighborhood men would return home on leave from military service. I noticed that June Baby and other young ladies were no longer interested in playing hide-and-seek, as they left us silly little boys bewildered and went on dates with soldiers and sailors. Few who have not had the experience can appreciate the feeling of abandonment felt, typically, by young males who have been discarded by their female contemporaries who have moved on.

The house on Fourth Avenue South was built on an incline and so had an area towards the rear that had about six feet of height clearance. Like my refuge on Thirteenth Street, it was a wonderful place to have some alone time and to reflect. There was about a ten-inch drainage pipe that I would sit on, sometimes reading, sometimes staring into space. It was the first time I began to be curious about my own sexuality. (Maybe it had to do with what I was reading.) By this time, I had not even heard of the word "masturbation." But the curiosity got the best of me, and before I realized what was happening, I experienced the painful surprise that would join my list of things for which to feel guilty. I was beginning to load up on such baggage. And I have learned that you don't get to unload guilt until you get old—when self assurance creeps in and guilt becomes something to get over.

I had not outgrown my tendency towards deviance outside of school either. (When would I learn?) A group of the most devilish of us boys would organize ourselves to shoplift for candy and other snacks from grocery stores on the way to school. We would assign someone the responsibility of distracting the storeowners while others of us would stuff our pockets with candies and cookies for which we really had no practical use. We would then give them away to other students just to prove that we were cool. Little did we know how ridiculously silly we must have seemed. A rather entrepreneurial activity that we tackled had to do with climbing magnolia trees in the parkways in front of people's houses and then going up to the front door and selling them to the homeowners for five or ten cents, with the promise that "they'll make your house smell really good." The big thrill for us was in knowing that we were selling people their own product. Now that I think of it, we were not really getting away with very much anyway, since they were glad to get them and probably wouldn't have climbed the trees to get them down themselves. Much of our senseless activity was mostly about drawing attention to ourselves. Never mind that it was negative attention to compensate for the lack of positive feedback.

The source of a part of the new status that our family enjoyed in Titusville had to do with our relationship with our more socially upscale kinfolks, the McKinneys. In the early years, we suffered the cruelest of indignities at the hands of the children and to a lesser extent from the parents. We would be given overripe produce from their grocery store. While I am certain that Mama might have had a bit of a problem with accepting the bad fruits and vegetables, along with meats that were just this side of rancid, I am also certain that she did what she had to do to feed her family. Of course, for Bay-Suh and me, this was a source of excruciating embarrassment. We visited their nice home on occasion where we were subjected to further insults, such as the time we were asked by our cousins to "Get off of our wealthy steps" (See cp-17,#39, 2008), as opposed to our "poor" steps, (See cp-17, #40, 2008).

In many ways, I have often perceived our family to have been dysfunctional. But there are degrees of dysfunction. With all of their advantages, our cousins' family had some major problems. They were smothered with "love," to the extent that they were spoiled rotten in those early years. Thanks to increased exposure to more peers in the real world, they tended, at least the girl, to make rapid adjustment to some semblance of normalcy in their later adolescent years. Theirs was a classic case of too much too soon. Massive overindulgence. The girl, Jean, was killed in an auto accident with a married man while away at college. Her brother, Harrison, though currently doing relatively well at the age of seventy-six in a care facility, never held a job (he didn't have to), never had an intimate relationship, and never made a complete recovery from the loss of his sister. As a matter of fact, he is the only survivor in a family previously anointed in excesses. I suppose there are worse things than being poor. I stay in contact with him from facility to facility and am blown away by his long-term memory. He winds up bringing me up to date on some issues that I've forgotten.

I eventually spent a lot of time "on the corner," (cp-8, #15), where the younger of us sat at the feet of the older males and listened to their bravado and boastfulness about their sexual exploits and conquests. And, not knowing any better, we believed them, only to discover later that they generally were lying through their teeth. "The corner" was where many of us first heard such colorful phrases, all spoken in the vernacular of the streets, as "He looks like a monkey fucking a football" when someone was bumbling with something. Or when someone was either left out or expected to be satisfied with the leavings, they were "sucking hind tit," like the pushed-aside runts in a litter of pups. Or in a downpour, in the presence of elderly women, "It's raining like a double-cunted cow pissing on a flat rock." Or more recently, William's message to potentially abusive companions for his daughters, "If you fuck with my daughter, you can put your head between your legs and kiss your ass goodbye." The phrases make me cringe when verbalized in polite company, but the message is usually very clear. And, of course, I would never utter them. Of course.

On the corner there was also a pharmacy with a nice little soda fountain. The Jones brothers owned it. Bobby Jones had been Mama's boyfriend in her late teens. Bay-Suh and I had wondered why she had opted for the two ill-chosen spouses she'd had. Bobby Jones was a handsome young man, articulate, and taught at our high school. He would look at me adoringly as he was handing me my ice cream cone and say, "You should have been my son." And as I fantasized about the possibility, I could also envision having unlimited access to ice cream and milk shakes. But, then, I would not be me.

I think that most children get embarrassed and feel uncomfortable when parents show sentimentality among themselves. And it gets even worse if a person is included who is not your parent. It gave me a very queasy feeling, an "I-just-want-to-get-out-of-here feeling" when I saw Mama slow dance with Mr. Napoleon. I felt somewhat better when she was alone, with her glass of bourbon, her seamed stockings rolled down below her knees, and her leg hung over the arm of the chair. Alone meant no complications. And without complications, maybe our parents would get back together again, the fantasy of most children of divorces.

After graduating from Washington Elementary School, the next venue would be Ullman Junior High School. Ullman has now become an integral part of The University of Alabama physical education department, a Forensics Anthropology Laboratory, and faculty offices. I think it was at Ullman that I began to become a real pain in the neck for the teachers and the principal, Mr. George Bell. This is where the serious admonishments began. On the one hand, every time I encountered Mr. Bell in the hall, he would automatically order me to "Go home!" Because of my track record, he assumed that I must have done something wrong; he wasn't taking any chances. On the other hand, I actually received some encouragement from a few teachers. It seemed that the encouragement came mostly from English teachers, something I could never understand. This would be a pattern throughout high school.

One day Mr. Bell came into the lunchroom and said, "I will give a quarter to anyone who can spell 'Yvonne' correctly." No one said anything, and I piped up "Y-V-O-N-N-E." I am certain that I was not the source he expected the answer from. But he gave me the quarter, turned on his heels and left—I think in a huff. The reason for his attitude was somewhat justified. I had perceived it to be my job to drive the teachers and principal to distraction and to keep my classmates rolling in the aisles. I think I almost succeeded at my own expense, though I received a modicum of respect and recognition from some teachers who also necessarily had to chastise me on occasion. One such occasion was when I was sitting in one of the double desks in the back of the classroom with a girl. I, as usual, was teasing her, and in order to impress her, I did what many young boys do to impress girls. I took out my wallet and made a point, surreptitiously, of allowing her to get a peek at the round imprint made by the condom, which was always there. The idea, of course, was to impress her that I was sexually active, which I wasn't. Nevertheless, Mrs. Hayes, an English teacher, caught me taking the condom out of the wallet and ordered me to the front of the room. I was required to stand facing the class holding the dirty (from handling) condom out, dangling it in the wind, as she continued to teach. The idea was to embarrass me. What she did not know was that the converse was true. I was in my heaven standing behind her, back against the blackboard, smiling at the class.

After leaving Ullman Junior High School, it was now time to move on to the big time at Parker High School for the final two years of secondary school. Parker High was known all over the south for its excellent educational and athletic programs. It has a rich history dating back to 1899, with its first class

Parker High School Band. Look for the clown. Margie Cotton in upper left corner. William seated just below her.

starting in 1900. Parker has turned out a number of outstanding profession-als now located throughout the country. Luminaries include Alma Powell, wife of the former Secretary of State. She is also the daughter of R. C. John-son, principal at Parker when I attended there from 1947 to 1949.

I know of no child who did not look forward, excitedly, to matriculating to Parker, with its marching band, of which I was a member, and its awesome football team, the Thundering Herd. I, personally, did not give an awful lot of thought to its academic excellence. I saw the opportunity to inflict damage on new unsuspecting staff. Equally important to me, though, was the opportunity to play saxophone in Parker's famous band. (Page 41). By now, my musical skills were such that I could assume a leadership role as I pretty quickly moved to first chair. Mr. Hudson, the band teacher, gave me a little bit of slack, mixed with some stern discipline, which pulled me a bit towards center. I could now begin a maturity growth spurt, though I still had enough deviance in me to cause problems. I could still find a few other delinquents who were open to senseless mischief, such as pilfering slices of pecan pie in the lunchroom and spiriting them out in the pockets of sport coats. Obviously, the coats would never be the same again. We were not the most forward-looking crew. But now my deviance was sporadic, and my heart was really not in it.

There was real school spirit at Parker. My earliest experience with pride came when I was issued my first beautiful purple and white band uniform, which my friends and I, including Bay-Suh, flaunted proudly on the public busses en route to engagements at football games and parades. We got to travel on occasion with the football team for away games. One such trip took us to Dothan, Alabama, a small town which, though it was not too very far away, seemed to me, like worlds away from Birmingham. I continued to feel the effects of a limited sphere of mobility, which, if taken to the extreme, can be debilitating. When asked today about other cities and towns in Alabama, even as an adult, I am at a loss, for the only thing I knew about Alabama was Birmingham. And the memories are not that fond, especially outside of our community. At that time I often wondered why anyone who was lucky enough to leave Birmingham would dare to return. This was, of course, from the mind of a young traumatized boy. But the trauma is still with me, and I find it very hard to forget those really negative experiences. Now I can understand, especially in Birmingham's present social climate, why some African Americans would choose to return. Their reasons revolve around nostalgia, disenchantment with conditions in the North and the West, and cheaper and better housing. But today's climate is not the climate of the 40s,

50s, and 60s. Parker High School was kind of an oasis that, according to our uninformed perspectives, was self-contained, with its own leaders and role models, who held high expectations for us. And we were never allowed to forget it.

We, especially young people, needed this uplifting environment, in light of all that was designed by the institutionalized system to destroy our self-concept, including the former constitutional three-fifths rule, which considered blacks as three-fifths of a person. But well into reconstruction and beyond, there was never any let-up in the South in general, and Birmingham in particular, to denigrate and instill the lowest possible self-concept in Blacks. Racist Whites were masters at degradation in every aspect of life. Everything was totally and brutally separate and unequal. The public transportation system was notorious for its "colored" and "white" seating arrangements, and caustic and mean drivers were charged with enforcing the ridiculous rules. Eating accommodations, drinking fountains, restrooms, and fitting rooms were not accessible to the Blacks that largely supported the economy of department stores. There were three "colored" movie houses, The Famous, The Frolic, and The Carver, for the use of Black folks. Other movie houses existed, but they were not open to Blacks. The exception would be The Lyric, which accommodated Blacks through a side door, leading to the balcony. Hiring practices were just as degrading. The few Blacks that worked in the department stores worked as maids and custodial personnel. The police force was totally white, with an absolutely racist "Commissioner of Public Safety" named Bull Connor, of police dogs and fire water cannon fame, running it. His primary purpose for being was to intimidate the Black community.

On a recent trip to Birmingham, I was struck by changing demographics, both positive and negative. The positive, the African-American leadership has done strikingly impressive work in re-configuring what I have often called the formerly most racist and violent city I have known. The dispersal of American-Americans beyond the central city was a welcomed change. Though racial issues seem to have improved, the violence and poverty that I witnessed on that recent visit seems to have increased. The demographic shift has spread poverty into neighborhoods which previously had some semblance of respectability. This was a major disappointment to me as I toured some of the nicer communities that I had known, even though I had not resided in them. In talking with a neighbor of Mama's on this trip, Jacqualine Bibb, (that's right, Jacqualine) I reflected on the depressing appearance and nature of African-American youth in the streets who seemed to be idle and prone to trouble. Jacqualine responded that you have to be careful about even making eye contact with them, for they are looking for any excuse to confront you violently. I was frustrated, however, because I was aware that what I was seeing was not all there was. Somewhere in Birmingham, people were living better, I was touring in areas with which I was familiar in childhood, and perhaps even back then there were areas totally alien to me. So, are there two Birminghams today, as there were when I was a child?

In visiting Kelly Ingram Park, which was the staging area for downtown demonstrations, along with Sixteenth Baptist Church, I sat on a park bench observing the wonderful sculptures of Bull Connor's police dogs, water cannons, and people daring to pray during the demonstration. Kelly Ingram Park is practically hallowed ground, and as I looked across the park, I observed four young men shooting dice behind a sculpture.

Given the culture that we were forced to endure, I often wonder out loud how we managed to survive and maintain a semblance of sanity. Those who rose above the fray and did extraordinarily well deserve the respect and admiration fit for saints. And there have been an exceptionally large number of African-Americans out of Birmingham who have done just that. I hope no one gets the idea that horrible treatment is the vehicle to success, for these successes are the exceptions. The larger percentage of the population does not make it, precisely because of their experiences. I often hear the question asked, "Why don't they (meaning my peers) pull themselves up by their bootstraps?" It sounds a little trite and redundant to say that perhaps they have no boots. What does make sense is that every group has the right to have mediocrity within its population, along with its achievers. All groups have representation at all levels of performance. At the advanced years in life, one's accumulation of "things" will tend to be subjugated to self-evaluation and the more meaningful gifts one has to offer to humankind. Probably, by this time one becomes convinced that the more lofty aspirations of early years are not achievable anyway, or they decrease in importance. And if in the process of moving through life you make a positive difference in someone else's life, then all is likely to be right with the world.

Unlike the baseless May Katherine affair, I would now fall head over heels in love with the most beautiful, stately, exotic girl I had ever known (my perspective). Her name was Margie Cotton. She was a couple of years ahead of me in school, but years ahead in maturity. I did everything possible to impress her. I would do and say smart-alecky things to get her attention. At night, I would walk the couple of blocks past her house just to be in her vicinity. In the meantime, I could only watch as she focused her attention on older males with whom she was more appropriately matched. The saddest part of the story is that she never knew, at that point, of my foolish feelings for her, for I was reluctant, for good reason, to express them for fear of being ridiculed. The whole notion of disclosure was absurd. Margie suffered a stroke many years later, after being married and having beautiful children who looked like her clones. I learned later that she had been rescued by her mother from an extremely abusive marriage. Someone once said that "Timing is Everything." When it was safe, several years ago, I had the good fortune to visit with her as she was confined to a wheelchair and to disclose my ridiculous feelings for her when I was a child. We recounted the carefree years of the late forties, remembering some of the jokes that were shared among groups of students on the way to school, had a few laughs, and a few years later, Margie died.

7

TUXEDO
JUNCTION

Several miles southwest of downtown Birmingham is a town called Ensley, where Mama's sister, Aunt Helen, and three of her children–Madeline, George, and Harold–lived. Her eldest son, Sam, was a former missing-in-action veteran, an educator, and a role model for those of us who followed. He died a very young man of 45, some years after getting out of the army, leaving behind a wife and two daughters, Janice and Wanda, whom he absolutely adored. Ensley had two claims to fame for African-Americans in Birmingham: the first was the dance hall and club at Tuxedo Junction (cp-10, #20) for which Erskine Hawkins, the renowned Birmingham trumpet player and big band leader, wrote the title piece we grew up on and played in our own junior high school jazz bands. The second claim to fame for Ensley was the only public swimming pool for Blacks in Birmingham, which meant that Black people from all parts of the city had to board public conveyances, for the most part, and travel great distances to get there, often transferring on busses and streetcars several times.

The youngest of my three cousins, Harold, was about my age, and we were the closest of them all. There seems to be the general opinion that only girls give serious thought to matters involving their aspirations for adult life, such as, family, children, relationships, careers, and general lifestyle. Harold and I had several discussions, while sitting on the curb, regarding our prognosis for the future, even as early as our short-pants days. But plans have a way of going awry, and I doubt if either of us got off the ground as we had hoped. We went so far as to list the desired mental and physical characteristics of our future wives. We would have a couple of children, a boy and a girl, with the boy being older (what a novel idea). We would have wonderful, lucrative careers and all the amenities, e.g., fine homes, nice cars, and other comforts, which, in retrospect, would not seem likely in 1940's Birmingham, Alabama for African-Americans. Like everyone else, we were victims of media's and storybooks' portrayal of ideal family life. This was another example of children's ignorance being bliss. As it turned out, Harold wound up in the Marine Corps, too, although our lives became disconnected, and I was not aware of his service until many years later.

I did not realize it at the time, but the move to Titusville situated us in an environment which would prove to be extremely advantageous, for we were now among families which encouraged children to do well, both academically and socially. The pervasiveness of musical training, though undetected by us children, produced multi-dimensional, largely egghead types, who probably could not qualify for more strenuous athletic activities like football or basketball. Our air of superiority and arrogance served as defense mechanisms to compensate for our physical inadequacies. After all, the jocks were thought to be not very bright. Our uncommon arrogance probably resulted from our own feelings of inadequacy. An inordinate number of our peers in the high school band went on to do well in the professions. The jocks probably had their share of successes as well. But we'd never admit it.

8

Jobs—
Well Kind of . . .

An important pattern began to emerge back when we lived on Thirteenth Street. I began to develop the makings of a strong work ethic, (in spite of several painful rough spots) which has stuck with me throughout my life. The ethic was not without its flaws. As a child, I was almost never without a job of some sort, but I was fired from more than half of them. Employers very soon discovered my immaturity and lack of productivity and let me go. What was amazing, though, was that I always managed to get another job the next day.

My very first "job" was without an employer. I was my own "boss," for I had built myself a shoeshine box, and, though I knew absolutely nothing about shoe care, I managed to pull it off. I think that many of my customers were simply being kind to me, an industrious young lad forgiven for his ineptness, as long as I did not ruin their shoes. Some of the shoes were quite fancy. There were the spectator styles, which typically were brown and white with many little holes along the brown, which had to be done meticulously with a matchstick one hole at a time. It took far more patience than I had, and I tended to get up some speed to get it over with. The outcome was something less than desirable. I soon began to feel that the work was degrading. For me, there was hardly anything more demoralizing than falling to one knee and cleaning and shining someone's shoes, and then being flipped a coin for my services. So I quit in order to seek more meaningful employment, which turned out to be as a delivery boy for Fagan's Bar-B-Q Shack. Fagan's was located in an alley, which was a hangout for partiers in the late evening. Today I think that a child would not be allowed to be in that sort of environment at all hours of the night. Fagan's also sold fish sandwiches, to which I was addicted, even though they used only cheap whiting fish. I think I ate more than I delivered.

My next employment was as a paperboy, delivering the only African-American newspaper in Birmingham at the time: *The Birmingham World*. The price for a newspaper was five-cents, which seemed exorbitant. My paper route was restricted to our immediate community, for the most part. Subscribers paid twenty-five cents per week for five newspapers. My biggest problem was that, very often, customers did not pay when due, which meant that I had to chase them down throughout the week. Sometimes they did not pay at all. And when they did pay, I would make a beeline to the nearest store to buy candy. I said that I was industrious, not frugal. At the end of my route on collection day, I would have nothing to show for the week's work except a sugar high and teeth that would be a dentist's dream, provided I had dental care. Which I didn't. After a spell, the newspaper business no longer seemed appealing, so I gave it up and moved on.

It is important to note that our community, Titusville, was virtually self-contained, from the view of a young teenager who could satisfy all of his needs within its boundaries. Obviously, this was not the case for the adults who generally had to venture into the outside world for employment and other commerce. What it amounted to was both *de jure* and *de facto* segregation. *De jure* because Birmingham's Jim Crow, or Separate but Equal Laws were always separate, but never equal, and *De facto* because circumstances, such as economics, levels of education, and the propensity to gravitate to those in the same boat, tended to push people together. But the preeminent factor was the law, which did an effective job of creating and maintaining unequal living conditions. Titusville was a cut above many other African-American communities at the time, though a significant cleavage existed between the "haves" and "have-nots" even there. African- American communities, unlike their white counterparts, threw everyone together, whether some could afford to live elsewhere or not. Once again, though, there are *blue skies* here as well. The self-contained community made it unnecessary to interface with the white world, only to be denigrated. The community provided opportunities for its members to develop leaders and to put their lives in a context with people with whom they would interact and, equally important, with people who really mattered in their daily lives. As would become obvious later in the Civil Rights Movement, the leadership seemed to revolve around church facilities and activities. Going downtown was a menacing experience, except for the Fourth Avenue district where the African-American businesses were located.

The major department stores and five-and ten-cent stores, while raking in massive amounts of money from African-American patrons, provided no services, e.g., changing rooms and eating facilities. In addition, African-Americans were greeted with contempt and scorn. I often wonder how people can possibly come out of these and other such experiences with good mental health and self-esteem. I am quite aware of the level of self-hate that permeated the minds of too many of us—until the Civil Rights Movement when Black became beautiful.

My next employment was as a delivery boy for Benny Coleman's Dry Cleaners on the Southside. I suppose it made some kind of cost-saving sense to have a boy delivering and picking up dry cleaning on a bicycle, but I managed to make it very inefficient. By the time I reached the customer's residence, the clothes had been mangled in the spokes of the bike's wheels and the greasy chain. I also did not manage my time very well. It took only the slightest distraction to get me off my route, returning to the shop late. It didn't help that my predecessor, a friend and classmate, had been very good at the same job for a long time and was good enough to hand it off to me when he moved on. Mr. Coleman had one of the few automobiles known to us at the time, and when he delivered me home for the last time, he very apologetically said, "Raymond, I don't think I'll be needing your services anymore." Bummer! Funny, I could understand why, but had the good sense to feel embarrassed, nonetheless.

Undeterred, I went on to my next job as a pin-setter at a bowling alley. The pins were set manually, before the advent of automatic machines, at least at this facility. It was grueling work, but the tips were good, and the camaraderie with the other boys, both Black and White, was even better. For a while, it was fun. Again, though, I began to perceive the work to be degrading, as people hurled bowling balls down the alley and it was the responsibility of the boys to get out of the way as pins flew all over the place. I began to get it when I could hear snickering from the bowlers as we scrambled for cover. So much for pin setting.

My next job was in the food services department at Hillman Hospital, where I was born. The older boys in the neighborhood, including William's brothers, had managed to get hired there, and William and I kind of rode in on their coattails. Our supervisor, a dietician, was a chubby Caucasian woman, Mrs. Caufield, who wore tight white uniforms and had the tendency to be overly chummy with the older boys. My own joy, however, came from being in the presence of so much food. I didn't know that there was such a quantity and variety of food on earth. And this is hospital food. Maybe this accounts for why even today I like hospital food while others around me detest it. When the older boys decided to leave, William and I left as well. There were many other worlds out there to be conquered.

I ventured into the downtown area for two of my childhood jobs. One was at Walt's Shell Service Station on First Street North just west of Sears, Roebuck & Co. (now a vacant lot). Walt was a kind of happy-go-lucky, cigar-smoking white transplant from Ohio who didn't appear to carry a lot of racist baggage. His primary employee was a middle-aged Black named Cleve, at whose feet I sat to learn my tasks. Cleve was the type of person you meet on the way to becoming. And you look back and wish you'd stayed in touch. He was gentle, steadfast, and wise. My job was to help hand-wash the cars, to pump gas, to clean windshields, to keep the soft drink case filled, and to help with oil changes and lubes. It was a good learning experience in basic auto care, though it would be years before I would own an automobile. But it was more rewarding to benefit from Cleve's wisdom. Typically, Cleve was as easy-going and patient as they come. Being very young and seeing the world through rose-colored glasses, I sometimes had to be reminded to not get upset by the racist incidents going on in my presence. Cleve had the notion that being cool meant that ultimately you would wind up on your two feet, even as others faltered. Although the idea is difficult to digest sometimes, Cleve seemed to be onto something.

The most memorable experience, though, was my first attempt at driving a car. One day, after washing, drying and tire-dressing a car, I thought I would put it in a parking spot on the premises. Mind you, I had never sat in the driver's seat in a car before and had no clue as to what I was doing. Just about every car back then was stick shift, which compounded my problem. I started the car somehow, not knowing the difference between a clutch and an accelerator, and took off. I also didn't know what and where the brake was. Bottom line, I wound up off the premises and into the middle of heavy traffic on First Avenue. It is said that God looks out for old folks and fools, and I wasn't very old at the time. I will never know how I managed to pull off the street into a pay-by-the-hour parking lot. I came to a dead stop about a foot from a red brick building. Cleve was furious and made me promise to never get behind the wheel of a car as long as I worked there. But his warning was totally unnecessary. I cringe when I think of the potential for disaster that day.

So now it was time to move on to cleaner and safer work. I got a job as a stock boy at the Junior Booterie, an up-scale children's shoe store farther downtown. I was glad that being hired didn't depend on such things as resumes or a track record. Otherwise, I would never be hired for any job. But I repeat, it was clean work and required a grasp of numbers, which was somewhat challenging. However, to work in the heart of the downtown area was not nearly as comfortable as back in our community. The patrons at the Junior Booterie were almost exclusively white. Attitudes shone through. And though not as intense as some of my previous experiences, a clear pattern was emerging. There was no place outside of Titusville where I would be made to feel comfortable and not be subjected to indignities, except at the two high schools, Ullman and Parker. Subconsciously, I began to plot an escape from Birmingham that would have to occur much later, at the right moment, upon graduation from high school.

For the time being, I decided that I should become my own boss again. On the backs of comic books were ads soliciting young people to become sales persons, hawking vegetable and flower seeds to their friends and neighbors. The idea was that the company would send you a supply of seeds, and depending upon the number of seeds you were able to sell, you could receive a range of gifts. The more you sold, the greater the gift. Well, sales didn't go too well for me and I was in a quandary. What do I do? Do I return the seeds and get nothing for my efforts? I had what I thought was a much better idea. The fourplex that we lived in on Fourth Avenue South was a massive house with an expansive backyard that extended all the way to the next street behind us. The soil was fertile, and none of our neighbors used any part of the yard. I would become a farmer. I tilled the soil with pick and hoe. I planted every package of seeds, including tomatoes, carrots, onions, beets, radishes, corn, and lettuce. This was not about entrepreneurship. I had not thought that far ahead. In fact, all of the produce was consumed by our household, including me, as I, while at play, would yank a carrot out of the ground, brush it off, and consume it on the spot. Beautiful, sweet, organic tomatoes were treated the same way. This venture had much to do with my aversion to chemical fertilizer use in produce today. There is obviously the difference in taste. But more importantly, there is a substantial difference in what we are doing to our bodies by ingesting chemicals that were designed primarily to produce greater quantity, not quality. I used no fertilizer at all. It would've cost money that I didn't have anyhow.

William and I began to scavenge for jobs in our neighborhood. Perhaps one of the most labor-intensive enterprises was the two of us digging pits for cesspool tanks, which is very similar to digging a grave. Unless a person has had the experience, it is hard to imagine using a pick to dig in red Alabama clay. It is analogous to the digging sticks used by hunting and gathering groups. The business ends of both tools were very inefficient, for they only turned over the amount of soil that fit the width of the very narrow tool. But we did it with gusto—two bare, bronze backs glistening in the brutal Alabama sun. In addition to the monetary pay we received, Mama would allow William and me to have a beer, one beer, after a good bath. To show what novices we were, it was simply the coldness and wetness of the beer that was so appealing. We actually poured the beer over ice in the glasses. Mama's position was that she'd much rather have us drinking beer in our house than "out in the streets." We were 16.

Now it was time for William and me to move into the big time. We could now work for his grandfather, who contracted to build fine homes. We worked along side the older boys at half their wages. They earned a dollar an hour, while we earned fifty-cents. At the time, twenty dollars per week was big money. Many grown men with family responsibilities earned no more than we. Mr. Garlington was in high demand, though he commanded higher rates for his work, which was a testament to the quality he insisted upon. Every one of us was required to do the best quality and most thorough work possible, and if one of the grownups passed by and noticed something being done improperly, we might receive a rap on the knuckles with a hammer handle and were required to take it apart and do it over. No reckless abandonment.

On two occasions I witnessed Grampa, as we all called him, upset. One occasion was my doing. (Wouldn't you know it?) I was on the roof working, but also fooling around (as usual), when all of a sudden I dropped my hammer, which found its mark on Mr. Hardy's head. Mr. Hardy was the gentleman in whose truck we were transported to and from jobs. At this point, Grampa was visibly upset, and we were transported from work to home. Grampa displayed an enormous amount of tolerance with us boys, and I was sometimes amazed at how quickly he recovered from some of the pranks and senseless accidents on his jobs. Consequently, the next day, we were back on the job. Grampa was the nearest thing I ever had to a Grampa, and I regarded him as such affectionately. Both of my real grandfathers died before I was born. With significant increase in longevity rates, young folks are so fortunate today to have grandparents around well into their own adulthood. But they have no basis for comparison and often do not appreciate that valuable resource.

The second occasion also happened on a job. Grampa had all the physical characteristics of a Caucasian, which was, and still is, not uncommon in Birmingham. I am certain that those characteristics must have caused a lot of confusion, especially for Whites. (We were used to such people in our midst, for once contaminated with an iota of African-American blood, a person is deemed African-American. It is called "The one-drop rule.") One day the homeowner with whom Grampa had contracted made a comment about these "fine nigger boys you've got working for you." Without hesitation, Grampa ordered everyone into the truck for the trip back home. I have noticed that none of the boys who worked for Grampa grew up to be unwilling to protect themselves in the clinches. All managed to hold tenaciously to principle.

Eventually, three or four of us struck out on our own and contracted to do small projects, such as garages and small outbuildings. Out of this grew a sense of independence and a "can-do" attitude, and for me, a lifelong fascination with close tolerance woodwork. In my final days in Birmingham, I did a few solo jobs, which I go back to check out on the rare occasions when I visit home. On my 2008 visit to Birmingham, I noticed that some of the work had been razed. The projects that still exist look good after more than half a century.

9

THE GOOD, THE BAD, THE UGLY

While still at Ullman Junior High School, I had to walk a couple of miles to school each day, and it would be where I would show off for the girls, especially Margie Cotton. In time, I came to realize that Margie was a lost cause. My aspirations were unrealistic. In spite of my peers' determination to set me up with the sassy Lizzie Bea, I was now attracted to a very pretty and intelligent girl in my class, Juliet Grattan. We formed a relationship in 1947 at Ullman that carried through our Parker High School years and would last until 1967. We were married in 1949. As with most children, especially adolescents, there is very little in childhood that is truly happy and not awkward. Once again, my fortitude and resolve would be tested, for Juliet was very much in demand. She was a shapely, voluptuous girl at a time when all of our hormones, including Juliet's, were running rampant. The competition was fierce, and I have never been convinced that I had enough going for me to beat out my adversaries, some of whom were older and certainly more psychologically mature than I. One was actually a college student who was home for the holidays. My ultimate "success" was probably more a matter of designs she had on me (for some strange reason) than any special qualities I possessed. Although I was far from popular among our peers, Bay-Suh was "Miss Everything." So any popularity accruing to us had to be the result of a very social, outgoing, achieving, good-looking young Miriam. Actually, I possessed absolutely none of those qualities and have managed to acquire only two of them to date, and good-looking and achieving are not the two. (And although I can be "social" and "outgoing," I learned only a few years ago that I am truly at heart an introvert.) Funny, but we biological brothers do not appreciate the beauty in our sisters until it is pointed out to us by others, and then we don't believe it. Why, they are simply girls and pesky at that.

And so, Juliet and I began a torrid relationship that took us to moonlit trysts in wooded areas, in the cemetery, or wherever those hormones would take us. We often went to house parties where almost exclusively slow dancing took place in darkened rooms. There were wall-to-wall warm teenage bodies gyrating to tunes such as "After Hours," a sensuous, pulsating piece, referred to as the "anthem" by our set. Such activities, while fun at the time, are loaded with potentially horrible long-term consequences, especially when done by immature, uninformed adolescents.

As things progressed, we became more and more careless, and the inevitable happened. We became more sophisticated in our choices of places to make "love," an act that always gave me extreme anxiety. I think the anxiety was born mostly of guilt. A woman, who owned a rather nice house, rented rooms by the hour for two dollars. Following in the footsteps of the older boys—William's brothers and cousins and their friends—Juliet and I began patronizing her place after late night parties. The most anxious of all these episodes was the night Juliet became pregnant. I remember it well, and I feel the pain whenever I recall that night. The pain continued in our lives for the next seventeen years. I have always wondered if the discord in our relationship began with that first misstep, though there were many others to follow.

Other missteps might include a community that tolerates a woman who would encourage underage customers to use her place. It would be impossible for the community to be unaware of what transpired in that house, with all the comings and goings. But she cannot be blamed for the entire debacle. It could be said that being in the confines of a house was perhaps a lot safer than the insecurity of the woods. A major misstep was for children, especially as immature as I was, to be turned out into the world with so little preparation. I don't remember any warnings or instructions from my parents, although it is true that I probably would not have listened. Remember the hormones? Parents typically did not communicate about such matters with their children in our communities.

So, Juliet and I got off on the wrong foot and things never corrected themselves. We were marched down to the courthouse by our mothers to be married in an elevator by a Jack-leg preacher, who just hung around the courthouse waiting for customers. Another misstep. This was a marriage that never should have happened. In that community at that time, it probably seemed like the proper thing to do. Even today, the debate continues as to the appropriateness of that practice.

The trauma of Juliet's pregnancy reverberated throughout the rest of my life, and certainly hers as well, for the issue was not one of blame, but one of ignorance on both sides. A bad matter was made worse because absolutely no preparation had been made for a very untimely situation. After the courthouse scene, we both retreated to our respective homes and I, for my part, continued to live the basically dependent life I'd always lived with my parents. Juliet's situation was probably much worse, for I could at least work at whatever job I happened to have at the time. And I could continue to attend school in my senior year, whereas she was allowed to finish school, but not allowed to walk at graduation. Juliet was a brilliant book-learning student, and I am sure her family had the highest expectations for her. With my meager income, I tried to contribute to her needs. Mama made a number of maternity dresses for her, including the pink gabardine one worn to the courthouse. Daddy, who had not been that consistent about the needs of Bay-Suh and me, would take supplies of groceries to her. What was that all about? Guilt? Or attempts at restitution for past sins?

10

LOOKING FOR
A WAY OUT

My Aunt Mary, the affluent and politically connected one, had arranged to intercede on our behalf in acquiring an apartment in the Smithfield projects. Though this may sound like nothing to make a big deal of, not just anyone could get into the Smithfield Projects—government projects built for low-income families. (cp-11, #22). You had to know someone, and Aunt Mary was the one to know. Many of the residents were a cut above the average poor family in Birmingham. But because income was so low for even the professionals, some of our teachers from Parker lived in the projects, which were across the street from the school. We had commitments from family members, including Aunt Mary, for apartment furnishings. But, for some reason, Juliet's mother decided to "turn up the screws" on me. At about that time, carpentry work dried up and, feeling a sense of responsibility, I began to panic and decided that, in the present environment, there was no way out except to head north to East Orange, New Jersey to an Aunt Missy, whose son is John Amos, the fine actor, who was just a scrawny kid when I lived with them. I worked at jobs in restaurants in Newark and learned that I was not really suited for the demands of the jobs. After a short stay in New Jersey, I felt the strong pull of Birmingham because of the baby, and it seemed that Juliet and I were on decent terms. But things were still stressful: no jobs and Juliet's mother. And so, William, being in the same boat, agreed that we should explore the Air Force. We went through the recruitment process and I was accepted, but William, because of a prominent scar on his face, was rejected. I was then shipped off to Lackland Air Force Base in San Antonio, Texas. Recruit training was actually kind of fun and exciting. But the Air Force was not accepting married recruits, so I claimed to be single. I got completely through recruit training when one day I was called to the squadron office and was told that they'd heard from my mother-in-law that my son, Ronnie, had been born to my wife, Juliet, and that I shouldn't be allowed to remain in the Air Force. I was given passage home with a general discharge. Another painful disappointment that has remained with me to this day. It never pays to speculate on the might-have-beens, but one wonders if things might have been different, positively, if the Air Force had panned out. Of course, the downside is that I would not have experienced the wonderful things that have transpired in life as I know it. I make it a point to never look back at the past too longingly, for the past cannot be relived.

New York, New York

Things in Birmingham were worse than ever. The economy had taken a tailspin. Juliet's mother had a bug somewhere and had what might have qualified as a notary who palmed himself off as a lawyer and made annoying attempts at harassment, which exacerbated an already tense situation. So now, I headed for Boston to be with an Uncle Thompson and Aunt Ethel (who had made the best milkshakes ever in Atlanta). Again, I worked at a restaurant, on Massachusetts Avenue, called The Chicken Shack. This time I think I got it right and was progressing with my work nicely. But Uncle Thompson was accustomed to the privacy of his own space and shared as much with Aunt Ethel. He simply didn't want me there. Coincidently, I received a call from my friend, William, who was situated in New York and invited me to "come on down." He had been residing with one of his older brother's friends, who were hooked up with the Harlem numbers racket, which was pretty much controlled by the Mafia. It was an exciting time. We had what seemed to us to be unlimited money. We slept in rooms that had pillowcases full of unaccounted for currency. When going out on the town, we simply had to grab handfuls of money, stuff our pockets, and hit the streets. Our jobs involved serving as runners (for me *déjà vu*), delivering betting slips, stuffing packets into hiding places, jumping over roofs, exercising discretion, and simply being deviant. The pay-off was a partying lifestyle unparalleled by many grown-ups. We hit all of the major jazz clubs, such as Bop City, Birdland, The Apollo, and The Savoy. At the age of nineteen, we shouldn't have been allowed in the establishments, drinking like fish, staying up all night. But no one seemed concerned.

The streets of Harlem were especially stimulating for two uninitiated boys from Alabama. But we made the adjustment rather smoothly and enjoyed the lack of structure, including meals taken at hot dog stands and an unforgettable take-out place called The Rotisserie. Everything in the vicinity of One Hundred Twenty-Fifth Street and Lenox Avenue was fast-paced and filled with all manner of people, well-dressed people, hustlers of several varieties, too-mature children, street vendors, and prostitutes, whom I'd never be able to identify. William was far more adept than I at recognizing the hustlers and scams, my innocence being a holdover from my more sheltered childhood. We managed to avert the dangers related to our jobs, such as law enforcement and the normal hazards of the streets. We were never in trouble with the law. Life was mostly fun and games and exposure to a life we'd never known and probably would never experience again.

In my Marriage and Family classes I try to impress upon parents, especially mothers, the tremendous amount of lifelong influence they are likely to have over their children's lives. Never has this been more apparent to me than in my exit from Harlem. After all, what could be more appealing to a young impetuous, wide-eyed youth than the absolute freedom and treachery found on the streets of Harlem? Enter the long arm of Mama. One morning, after being up all night partying non-stop, William and I were having breakfast in a restaurant when suddenly, through blood-shot, gravelly eyes, we looked at each other knowingly and at the same moment seemed to acknowledge that we'd probably gone too far, with impunity, and needed to get back to something near reality. After all, what would our folks think if they knew what we were doing? They'd kill us. And what about our responsibilities back home? Something in our upbringing told us that what we really needed was a good dose of discipline. So, we finished our breakfast, hailed a taxi, and headed for 90 Church Street in Manhattan to the Marine Corps Recruiting Station. This time, it worked. They accepted us both, with the understanding that we were both single. Not. Neither.

11

FROM THE HALLS

OF . . .

I am certain that those who are aware but feign ignorance understand that the vast numbers of poor and unemployed people who wind up in the military do so because there are few options open to them in civilian life. Southerners seem to be overrepresented in all the branches, but especially the Marine Corps and the Army. As a result, an inevitable culture too often emerges in the ranks. Many times people from desperate origins find themselves in positions of authority, something they've never experienced before. They learn quickly to use and abuse it. Perhaps now is a good time to look at the obituaries of the young men and women who have died in a seriously questionable war in Iraq, to get a feel for the ages, the races, the ethnicities, and the hometowns of the deceased. The pattern is so obvious that one would need to either reside on another planet or be in complete denial with regard to the facts.

So, we, along with a cadre of young New Yorkers, found ourselves on a train heading for Parris Island, South Carolina. Maybe the experience at Lackland Air Force Recruit Training had been exciting and fun. But at Parris Island, we had no idea what we were getting ourselves into. In addition to recognizing that we needed the discipline, as kids we were also influenced by military movies starring John Wayne, John Wayne who never served a day in the military due to deferments, but was a movie military hero. A farce. But we were just as gullible and susceptible as all other old and young people, especially during the war years. And so, it was about "fixed bayonets!" "Over the top!" And "Hot machine gun barrels burning the skin from your palms." How exciting! But now we were to learn that there was more to it than the dress blues shown on recruitment posters. We would get them, but we would pay dearly for them.

The trip from New York to Parris Island was in itself an eye-opener. We were immersed in a diverse culture consisting of five African-Americans, an equal number of Jews, a larger percentage of German extraction, a couple of Puerto Ricans, and four Italian-Americans. We began to get a feel for what life would be like in this mix. Instead of superiority being based solely on physical differences, bravado and claims of superior knowledge and experience were staked out for some, while others were vilified (in jest) and almost brought to tears. It was our first emersion into a truly integrated culture. It was weird that we did not feel at a disadvantage, not in spite of but because of our experiences at Parker High and our community in Titusville. But boot camp is an excellent equalizer. And an amazing transformation was about to take place.

Parris Island is just that—an island accessible by rail and vehicles through swamps. Talk about isolation! It has successfully trained thousands of recruits from the early part of the 1900's, though it has been in existence since the late 1800's. I facetiously refer to Parris Island as the real boot camp, as opposed to San Diego, which I saw, and continue to see, as sunglass-wearing, duck-tailed "Hollywood Marines." Parris Island was brutal. It is what "Full Metal Jacket" is about, actually where it was filmed. Violence perpetrated on the recruits was the rule. Drill instructors must have had a laundry list of ways to physically harm the neophytes. Concerns for their good health and safety seemed non-existent. Witness the case of Staff Sergeant Matthew C. McKeon, who marched a platoon into a swamp at Ribbon Creek where six recruits died. The rule in the Marine Corps is to obey orders without question, which meant that no recruit up front was going to say, "but Sergeant, we're approaching a dangerous situation!" So much for unquestioned compliance, even when lives are at stake. Psychological abuse was also at work 24/7. Religious persecution was fairly routine. The few recruits who expressed the desire to attend chapel were ridiculed and ostracized. They were often referred to by the drill instructors as "church boys," which would cause them to dig deeply into their faiths to persist in attendance. The weaker or more intimidated ones were more likely to refrain from drawing attention to themselves by requesting to attend services.

William certainly was not weak. Because he tended to manipulate situations, he was singled out by the drill instructor and derisively referred to as "Sunshine." This manifested itself clearly, as there were only a handful of African-Americans among us. But he did not cave. I often wondered, however, if that treatment didn't form his negative view of the entire experience, for it would dog him for the duration of his years abroad.

The whole purpose of Marine Corps boot camp is to take large numbers of undisciplined young men and move them through the resocialization process. This entails having them unlearn what they have already learned and replacing it with something believed to be a better alternative, which in this case would be Marine Corps doctrine, manifested in the Marine Corps Manual. It is said that the process is almost always painful and seldom completely successful because it attacks many very basic values learned at the knees of parents and family and held to be dear. The transformation is often temporary and made with reluctance. The Marines, though, like to believe in the dictum, "Once a Marine, always a Marine." It all depends on the susceptibility of the individual. Those with resolve are more capable of "playing the game" or doing what they have to do to get through the process. Those without the strength, or who have the need to fill voids in their lives, are more likely to buy into the process for the long-term or to become "lifers." Of course, there is the element of patriotism, which may develop before, but mostly after, indoctrination.

Parker High's influence continued to be felt, even in boot camp, as William and I learned that the basic principles involving pride and positive self-concept became a part of our make-up, and we quickly learned that suffering from what we had heard to be "education inferior to that offered in northern schools" was not the case at all. In fact, our backgrounds seemed to make us better prepared to deal with the requirements of service testing. We had always heard of the enormous range and variety in northern curriculum, many subjects that we had seldom heard of. And the range was there. The difference was that while they were armed with some knowledge in an amazing number of exotic and eclectic areas, our strength lay in a far better grasp of the basics, which were handled with extreme intensity. Remember Mrs. Boyd? The southern dialect, which has often been denigrated in literature and other art forms, played out in such a way as to respond more readily to requirements demanding standardizations. We did well. And the pattern was established for the remainder of our service experience.

I have almost always believed that being born the "scroonchie" baby has cost me dearly. Massive discourse exists on the advantages accruing to individuals who are tall, including evidence that they are more likely to be assigned leadership roles. The arbitrariness of how each of us is assigned our unique physical characteristics has both fascinated and confounded me, in light of the advantages and disadvantages that accompany such designations. Witness, for example, Mama's tendency to be overly protective of me, which then on occasion led to early childhood arrested development, both physical and mental. But, fortunately, I got over it. Equally fascinating is the fact that little could have been done to change the course of my physical development. Basically, I was what I was destined to be. "Scroonchie." But, then, take a look at the benefits that often accrue to a specimen just because of physical size and prowess, even when there's nothing else.

Initially, and for a long time, I felt some bitterness and a hopeless level of unfairness with the way things were structured, so that one's fate depends quite seriously on the accident of birth. The *blue skies*, however, reveal that the pendulum swings both ways. Some are born with certain talents, others with different ones, though more or less as lucrative. Random means just that. Any one of us could have been dealt a different hand. The key, of course, is what you do with what you are given.

Athleticism has been a major route out of the despair of poverty and disenfranchisement for African-Americans. It has worked both for and against us. With virtually all other avenues closed to us, especially in the sciences and business, and especially in times past, sports and entertainment have been our vehicles. But it has left too many of us depending solely on those vehicles for the trip to prosperity. In the meantime, the all-too-important safety net of substance is often forgotten and is left behind. I have had the marvelous opportunity to work with young African-American male youths, both in advisor capacities in college and in mentoring and tutoring in the community. A serious problem among them that I encountered repeatedly was the belief that all they needed for success is to be able to "slam-dunk," "clothes-line," and "outrun the world." I can't recall the number of times I heard this response to my questions regarding focus, motivation, and goals: "I really don't need all of this stuff. I'm going to be a pro," as they swaggered around bouncing basketballs. What are the odds? And how long lasting is the ride? My son-in-law, Sean, in his youth was one of the thousands of young athletes with all the moves, agility, and motivation to be highly successful in professional basketball. He has the high school and college track record to prove it. What he does not have is the all-important Masai warrior type height that scouts look for. He is 5 foot, 9 inches tall. How many 5 foot, 7 inch Spud Webbs are likely to have extensive careers with the Atlanta and Sacramento NBA teams?

It makes absolutely good economic sense to avail oneself of whatever resources are accessible to pursue college careers, especially those who are overrepresented among the impoverished. But a large part of the potential for success in those pursuits lies in the motivation to look beyond careers which are destined to be all too brief. My advice to young men has always been, "That's all well and good. Test the waters. Find out what it can do for you. But whatever you do, bring your education along with you. The certainty is that whatever the outcome, you'll need it." Needless to say, most do not heed such warnings until it is too late.

William and I were among the first "Smurfs" allowed into the Marine Corps. Prior to our enlistments, there had been such things as height requirements, obviously to fit the recruitment poster image with the Aryan stock in dress blues. But I suppose they had run out of big people who were willing to volunteer for what was demanded. The test, now, was to see how little people measured up. We little people, all of us new ones, quickly established that, in this instance, size didn't really matter. Maybe it was pure determination to prove the point, but in long forced marches, carrying what seemed like tons of equipment, we tended to prevail when many of the brutes were dropping like flies. We generally did much better with calisthenics than they.

An important and memorable aside for one so far removed from the comfort and security of home: one *blue skies* experience while I was in boot camp was the arrival of a package on my birthday from Mama containing fried chicken (which serves to feed the stereotype) and homemade biscuits—through the mails. Nothing ever, ever compared with that taste of "home."

Though no real Marine wants to admit it, the U.S. Marine Corps is a branch of the U.S. Navy, and the disdain that Marines and sailors have for each other is legendary. Fights aboard ship and on liberty and incessant name-calling were all a part of the game. Marines were referred to as Jar-Heads or Sea-Going Bellhops. Sailors were called Swab-Jockeys with cute little rows of buttons on their britches. It was about boys being boys. While females are typically about cooperation and sensitivity, boys are about competition. "Anything you can do, I can do better." Or "Mine is bigger than yours." Nowhere was this tug-o-war more pronounced. So, having a relevant symbiotic relationship with the Navy, a requirement, as with the Navy, is that members prove aquatic skills. This means being able to survive in the water with those tons of gear. I absolutely never pulled it off. I never learned to swim and wondered why I managed to be retained for years. This was another job Birmingham did on me by having no provisions for developing such skills, except for Munga or distant travel, neither of which was an option as far as I was concerned.

And so, a very successful boot camp came to an end. We were the Honor Platoon. I had moved through the most demanding recruit training to be found anywhere. I was still "scroonchie." I had actually excelled in every phase of training—pistol expert, rifle marksman, etc., all except swimming. These qualities soon became crucial because at the end of boot training, Parris Island received a letter from Juliet's mother informing them that I was married and should not be allowed to remain in the service. I was now referred to by the staff as "the delinquent." I was called to the office and queried about my assessment of the situation and actually asked what I wanted to do. This was the first time since enlisting that my input had been sought. By now, I was feeling pretty good about my accomplishments and was in no hurry to give it all up. And so, I indicated that I had no interest in being discharged. There began a very long-term relationship, one that really should not have lasted so long.

We new recruits left New York for Parris Island as an integrated bunch, with a massive amount of racial and ethnic diversity. We learned to get along well together, gaining appreciation of the various cultural backgrounds. We quickly picked up on the need to co-exist peacefully, since we were all in the same boat. Misery and depersonalization were the common denominator, which is an effective equalizer. But, while we arrived as interracial ragamuffins, after graduation we went our separate ways to different permanent duty stations. Maybe it was coincidental, but all African-Americans wound up at Camp Le Jeune, North Carolina. What's more, we all ended up in the same platoon, a segregated outfit dedicated primarily to cargo handling. I seriously doubt that it was coincidental.

On the surface, this has to seem like a depressing scenario. And it was. But there were redeeming consequences as well. The negative, serious, and long-term social and political results reflected the accepted way that African-Americans have been regarded and, therefore, treated in this society at large. There are few comfort zones, however, as warm and fuzzy as being in the company of fellow travelers, people who share your concerns and problems and who have had to discover creative ways of dealing with them. The wonderful sharing of typically southern dialect, jokes, and values not found elsewhere made the negative parts endurable. As most African-Americans are aware, there are few things as soothing as shifting into the cadence, and even denigrated usage, that make us feel as one. The beauty of it all, though, is that we also know how to make the necessary adjustments as needed. Our common ground is what helps to sustain us.

The downside of the separation at Le Jeune was its blatant racism, which was the order of the day. In retrospect, the ratio of whites, especially southern whites, to blacks was overwhelming, which then accounted for the oppressive structure of the organization and the relationships within it. Decent grade or rank was not to be found among those in our unit. Leadership roles were given to young whites (sometimes not so well seasoned), who then had to be trained by their African-American subordinates. As a result of President Harry S. Truman's executive order 9981 in 1948, the armed forces were to take the leadership role in integrating federal employment, Executive Order 9980. We now had a major problem because the military, especially the Marine Corps, was not the best role model. Total dissolution of segregated military units did not occur until 1954.

The highest-ranking African-American present at my new duty station at Camp Le Jeune was an amazingly talented staff sergeant named Al Alberts.

Although he was put in the unenviable position of having to direct the activities of rather hardened and disgruntled brothers, he had a way of eliciting uncommon cooperation and respect from them. The disgruntlement was the result of knowing that there was nothing anywhere near a level playing field. It was virtually impossible to make normal progress with regards to promotions. Because of the affront to the men's basic manhood and the tendency to develop "I don't give a damn" attitudes, the situation was unappealing, discouraging, and depressing. Needless to say, there was no such thing as an African-American commissioned officer in our ranks, though history would later prove that there were a number of us who were deserving. The floodgates would not open for some time to come, after I made the decision to remove myself from a situation that did not serve my best interests.

Because we, William and I, were among the first "little people" to enlist, we were fodder for harassment and ridicule by those already in residence. Verbal abuse and denigrating jokes were the order of the day, at which they were very skillful. William and I soon learned of the necessity to give it back—with our small voices. And we became pretty good at it. We learned that the best defense is a good offense, and soon the others lightened up a bit.

Perhaps because of the stressful conditions, and the need to strike out at someone, there were often beefs, which eventually led to fist-fights. It was a microcosm of society at large, as well as prison mentality, where, because it is not possible to turn on oppressors, the troops turned on each other. It was another example of black-on-black violence. I learned the hard way about how that process worked. Somehow, I got into a minor argument with a young New Yorker. To this day, I can't remember what it was all about. Being unsuspecting, and thinking that it was just about words, I was shocked when I was belted in the mouth without warning, losing two teeth. A pattern was beginning to emerge once again, for I had flashbacks to the "T" Johnson incident in the eighth grade, where I lost total control and had no idea of what I did after the initial shock. "T" Johnson got off lightly. This had the potential to have far more serious consequences. We were located on the second floor of our wing of the barracks. When I became cognizant of where I was and what I was doing, I had the other person hanging out of the window, ready to drop him onto the pavement below. Because all of us were in the same horrible boat, there was never a report filed, and I heard from the older ones what a "wonderful job" I'd done. What they didn't know was that it was because I was completely out of my head and would not, and probably could not, have done it if I had given it rational thought. The positive consequences coming out of this were two: (1) the realization that I cannot allow myself to lose control and (2) that the best antidote to doing so is to give serious thought to what is appropriate reaction to situations *before* they occur so that it does not become necessary under duress. Although this does not always work, at the very least I am reminded to back off and give myself space to regroup. I am a little guy, and I could get hurt. In retrospect, however, there were occasions in my life when I have wished that I could have reacted more emotionally than rationally. Though others have been successful with more violent reactions, I am convinced that given my luck, consequences would have been far graver for me.

12

SAN DIEGO

My time spent at Camp Le Jeune was too brief. I really did not have the opportunity to experience liberty in Jacksonville more than three or four times. Being the novice, there really was not very much for me there. But, being the novice and coming out of Birmingham, I was fascinated by the beach. I made countless trips to Onslow Beach where I simply "laid-out" in my canary yellow swim trunks. All was pretty much right with the world, for now, and for the first time in a long period, I had the opportunity to contemplate the future. I foresaw having an intact family, not knowing what that would mean in the Marine Corps. I imagined base housing, with Juliet and Ronnie, our first-born. I, of course, was very encouraged with the notion that I would have steady income with which to support a small family, although I had no idea of how tight things would be. And so, I would lie on the beach and dream.

Somewhere at Headquarters, Marine Corps, a different set of plans were not only being contemplated, but also acted upon. One day, after a full day at Onslow Beach, I returned to the barracks to learn that Korea was calling. The next thing I knew, our all-black, intact unit, the Second Combat Service Group, was on a troop train heading west to California. Me, without my two front teeth and clueless as to what had happened to my dreams.

I kind of got a lump in my throat when the troop train passed through Birmingham, halting momentarily for some reason. I think that it must have been about frustrating me. So near and yet so far. The trip west didn't make things any better: thousands of Marines with their gear stuffed like sardines into a long line of human cargo containers called passenger trains. The most was made of a worst-case scenario, and the jokes, songs, and lies cascaded from coast to coast. The trip was made in the middle of summer, which was unbelievably hot and sticky, and made almost intolerable by an inoperative air conditioning system all the way through Texas. I was struck by the way my companions got through the ordeal with humor and without mention of the conditions. I supposed that a hot, testosterone packed environment was a small matter compared to what these men had had to deal with throughout their miserable lives. Struggle builds character.

Our arrival in San Diego was my introduction to what would become an almost lifelong relationship with California. After Birmingham, Boston, New York, South Carolina, and North Carolina, the palm trees and exquisite weather of San Diego seemed like paradise to me. I imagine millions of people have shared that experience as they moved through California, across the Pacific towards Asia, promising themselves a place in the sun when they return. The attraction would be especially big for African-Americans in the 1950s when racial turmoil in the South was at its worse. California was rumored to be the Promised Land for Blacks. They were to learn differently later. The attention, by this time, had turned to a great extent away from the Northeast—New York, Chicago, Detroit, and Pennsylvania. California's appeal was not restricted to Blacks. Whites coming out of the cold climes of New England and the heat and humidity in the south also asked themselves the proverbial question: "Why am I dealing with unappealing elements and issues back home? I could get used to this in a heartbeat."

There was no opportunity for sightseeing in San Diego. We were totally restricted to venues and preparations designed to get ready for something that I still was incapable of comprehending. We were billeted in temporary housing, which should have been indicative of some ominous future move. But, oh no. I thought, what a wonderful opportunity in preparation for deployment to further play "poop and snoop," as we had done in boot camp. The rifle range at Camp Pendleton was more fun and games, without the stress felt in boot camp where actually I had done very well. I also did myself proud with the pistol and carbine, not understanding that in the near future I would need that expertise.

Many of the old-timers among us were familiar with the west coast area and all the places that we would not have the opportunity to explore. They had served in several southern California units before. It was interesting to watch reunion after reunion as old friends met. The difficulties that African-American servicemen face in the larger community are legendary. So, here was the sharing of experiences and the wisdom to survive both on and off military installations. There was the understanding that as one moves about this country, there are routes not to be taken. There was a fragmented network of places where accommodations might be expected. There were other places to stay away from altogether. Families traveling from duty station to duty station, on official orders, often had to sleep in their cars and get take-out food through the back door from segregated eateries. Any rational person would have a difficult time putting reason together with fact in the sort of treatment afforded African-Americans in the service of this country.

The networking did not stop at the sharing of information. Being the novice, I was amazed that there was such ready familiarity among the men. It was as though they'd seen one another only yesterday. It soon became obvious that all African-American Marines knew all other African-American Marines. After all, their numbers were small, since the welcome mat had not been out for their enlistment very long. The downside of the integration process that followed later was that we became splintered, which is the way things should have been all along. The upside was that by 1952, our unit was broken up and people were dispersed and dispatched to do things more commensurate with their interests and abilities. It was a long time coming, and there were further indignities to be dealt with for several years.

13

KOBE, JAPAN

The concept of inclusion hadn't happened yet, as we found ourselves board-ing a troop ship for parts not exactly known. It was a harrowing voyage that explained all the reasons why, for me, enlistment into the Navy would have been a big mistake. The ship departed from Broadway Pier in San Diego and would take a total of twenty-two days to reach our destination: Kobe, Japan. The twenty-two days were necessary because, under hostile conditions, it was not smart to travel in a straight line. And so, the ship zigzagged across the Pacific. The time factor was not our major problem. The conditions aboard ship were miserable for landlubbers not comfortable in cramped spaces. The smell of the fumes from the fuel for twenty-two days was un-bearable, and, of course, there was massive seasickness and vomiting among us for the duration of the trip, all of which rendered the better-than-average military food a virtual waste. There was more than the normal antagonism between the ship's company and the Marines who were their passengers.

Twenty-two days is a good bit of time to spend doing nothing. So, some-where in the heavens, someone decided that we could benefit from work-shops of all sorts. There were sessions to orient the troops to the places they could expect to find themselves visiting. Some basic things that should not be done were shared. Respect the culture. Forget about having conquered this population in World War II. Recognize and show appreciation for things deemed sacred to the hosts. Don't be the "Ugly American." In other words, be gracious guests. Pretty stimulating stuff for a bunch of bored and horny jarheads that are sitting dead on "full." On more than one occasion, at the end of a workshop, the inevitable question was asked by some eager young trooper, "Yes, but what about the women?" And it was clear that it really did not matter what women. Friendly women. Enemy women. The prevailing thought was that if you stood them all on their heads, they were all pretty much the same. Ours was a crude bunch.

We saw absolutely no land for the entire trip. I recalled, "Water, water everywhere, /Nor any drop to drink," from Samuel Taylor Coleridge. We passed the time doing meaningless things. We washed our clothes until they couldn't stand it anymore. A particularly highly placed value among Ma-rines was to exhibit seniority by appearing to be an "old salt." One way to do this was to bleach one's utility clothing until they were almost white. And it helped if they were also tattered. We spent a lot of time aft with clothes tied to a rope and pulled along in the salt water of the ship's wake.

There was also a higher than usual amount of gambling, supposedly to pass the time. But it was interesting that the winners were always the same two or three people who were skillful at poker, blackjack, and craps. Some came away extremely enriched, while others could hardly wait for the next payday. Some had concluded that there was a good chance that they would never have the opportunity to spend their money anyway, considering speculation as to where we were headed.

After so much time at sea, the very first sight of land was both unbelievably beautiful and foreboding. Beautiful because it had been so long since we'd seen land, and the skyline was Kobe, Japan. Foreboding because we were not too far removed in 1950 from the World War II years, and Japan was this country's enemy for four and a half years. All of our society had been so thoroughly indoctrinated that in spite of their defeat in World War II, Japan looked like enemy territory. And do I dare go ashore in enemy territory with two front teeth missing?

Kobe, Japan turned out to be an experience of a lifetime. This first, brief visit was one of two that I would experience, the second being longer and more involved. It was a port city of a million and a quarter people, known for its superb Kobe beef. Kobe was unique in that, unlike many other Japanese cities, it went unscathed during the war. The result was that it did not seem like a hostile city. More importantly, its people were far from hostile, though maybe they should have been, given the behavior of many of our servicemen as they roamed the streets sometimes in drunken, carefree rampages. The Army was already established in Kobe, with its several camps situated throughout the city. The Marines were guests who found accommodations far superior to what we were accustomed to. The food was wonderful. The living quarters were unlike anything we'd known, bordering on civilian standards. In the several times that our service branches found ourselves co-mingled, we quickly learned that the Army, Navy, and Air Force lived much better lives than the almost purely "grunt" nature of Marine Corps' existence. These differences would continue to emerge during the future military campaigns in Korea, as we raided their supply depots for items that were totally alien to us. Wonderful boots. Snazzy clothing. Brand new .45 automatic pistols, still packed in Cosmoline. We Marines felt like ragamuffins compared to the Army personnel.

The first stop in Kobe, being a staging area for the Inchon Landing in Korea, meant that we were confined to our billeting, surrounded by chain link and barbed wire fences. The local citizens would come to the fencing and interact with us, apparently as curious about us as we were about them. The confinement was for security purposes, although we were so much in the dark about

Me in Kobe, Japan on the way to the Inchon Landing.

our ultimate destination that there was nothing in the way of information that we might have shared with them anyway. Conversely, they knew all about what we were up to and when and where we were going. They were a good-natured people who seemed to belie the stereotype of vanquished, bitter survivors of a prolonged World War II, which had ended only five years earlier. I particularly remember a teen-aged girl who would kid me about my two missing teeth by simulating yanking them out. It must have really been amusing to her, for she would make it a point to be there day after day to antagonize and humiliate me. What she did not know was that membership in my outfit meant that I had been done by the masters, and no amount of kidding could surpass what the guys in the barracks did to me. This was my first exposure to and appreciation for the Japanese sense of humor. The rap on Asians, in general, was that they were stoic, humorless, and without passion. Herein lays the danger of stereotypes. First of all, it is ludicrous to categorize all Asian cultures as one, for there are vast differences in the various histories and worldviews among the various Asian cultures. My own development was unfolding step by step as each new exposure penetrated my senses. I was growing and was unaware of it. This was good stuff for one who, without knowing, would eventually become a professor of Anthropology. The combination of New York, boot camp, and Asia would become the backdrop for my fascination with cultural differences and how they intersect, for better or worse.

Towards furthering my understanding of cultural similarities and differences, I spent much of my down time in the company of a Chinese family in Kobe who were as welcoming and accommodating as one could imagine. We often think of racial and ethnic discrimination and prejudice being unique to our U.S. society, without considering the dynamics between and among other cultures. I was made aware of the unrelenting subjugation of the Chinese population residing in Japan. I even wondered why they bothered to live there, given those circumstances. Kind of like Blacks living in Birmingham. Why would those who could escape choose to remain? Could their treatment have anything to do with the history of the conflict among the Asian nations in the region? Japan dominated the region mercilessly for extended periods, and it seemed that neither the vanquisher nor the vanquished have forgotten that history. It is analogous to mentalities in the United States of those who were enslaved and those who were the beneficiaries of slavery. To date, neither group has forgotten previous conditions of servitude.

That history in our country has created awkward situations for people like me when abroad. I have had the uneasy experience in Japan of being called upon in private conversations with my Japanese counterparts to describe or explain race relations in the United States. I was always aware that individuals were asking questions for which they already knew the answers. And I had no desire to protect this country from such inquiries. I did, however, feel that it was our problem and not someone's who could or would not do anything to rectify it anyway. It was in the fifties and the entire world was aware of what was going on in the United States. It was a major source of embarrassment for American Whites transacting business with foreign interests. Another of my objections to such inquiries had to do with my own knowledge that those who inquire have done nothing to clean their own problems with racism. The treatment of Chinese residents in Japan, for example. I had the confidence that African-Americans had the wherewithal to deal with the inequities they faced back home, although it continues to be a work in progress.

It soon became clear that Kobe was the staging area for an ominous upcoming event. Even an uninitiated, immature adventurer such as I knew from the rather intense preparations everywhere we looked that things were getting serious. However, I was not bright enough to be concerned. After all, this couldn't be any worse than boot camp, could it? Hadn't I virtually aced everything they'd thrown at me and emerged unscathed? As it turned out, I had many more lessons to learn. And so, we departed from Kobe to a destination that would impact my very being for the rest of my life. It was the Inchon Landing in Korea that took place on the morning and afternoon of September 15, 1950. But, what is this? The vessel we boarded, with thousands of tons of equipment and supplies was not only a troop transporter, but a landing craft, an LCVP (Landing Craft, Vehicle/Personnel). The ships carried more than tanks. They carried us as well.

14

INCHON!

I suppose for all of us it is difficult to pinpoint the major transitions or turning points in our lives. First of all, I doubt that we are always sophisticated enough to see the significance of them, except in retrospect. And, of course, often it is the sum of several events in our lives that makes us who we are. Here, at the tender age of nineteen, I was about to be involved in a major invasion (actually, several). And as serious as this would prove to be, because I had not gone through the combat experience yet, this one seemed to pale by comparison to the dramatic warfare seen in the movies. Today as I begin to pile one negative experience atop another, I realize that, cumulatively, I've already been traumatized sufficiently to begin to shape the persona that is me. The poverty in a land of plenty, an abusive father and step-father, the petty theft experiences, the beatings at the hands of neighborhood kids, the embarrassment heaped upon Mama resulting from my behavior in school, the encounter with the man who stuck a gun in my face, the discharge from the Air Force after completing recruit training. But perhaps the greatest blow resulted from, without having a clue of what we were getting into, Juliet's pregnancy. That event would start a chain of events that would define the fate of too many lives—innocent and otherwise. But there are always *blue skies*, and my next venture would set me up to transition into adulthood, and out of negativity and despair I acquired the tendency to look for the brighter sides of even the bleakest situations. In spite of skeptics' outlook on my optimism, my stance, in the interest of good mental health, has served me well.

So, how could a full-out war possibly have positive consequences for a young wild-eyed nineteen-year-old? Ignorance proved to be an asset and my salvation. The initial stages of the invasion did little to impress upon me the seriousness of where we were and what we were doing. It all seemed so much like cowboys and Indians and childhood war games. It mirrored the many World War II movies that I had so thoroughly enjoyed as a child. How many times had I seen landing craft open their gigantic mouths and spit out Marines at port arms and fixed bayonet onto enemy beaches? And how many air assaults by low-flying Marine aircraft had I witnessed as I sat in the Frolic and the Famous movie houses in Birmingham? And hadn't our guys always won the day, with relatively few casualties?

So secure was I in the belief that this was no different and was pretty much business as usual that in the midst of the landing, I was topside of the landing craft, leaning on the rail, enjoying the scenery as our planes strafed enemy-held positions, watching the USS Missouri, the "Mighty Mo," bombard the shore in the "softening-up process, and savoring the excitement of what sounded like small arms fire pinging against the hull of our ship. Orange tracer bullets flew in all directions, as mortar rounds landed all around small craft heading for the beach. But it was all okay, because I had a ringside seat for this dream come true. I wondered why no one else was on deck to witness so rare a spectacle. I was shaken out of my reverie by the gravelly voice of a salty old gunnery sergeant, from some hidden position, who yelled, "You stupid little bastard, get your ass below deck before you won't have one to lose!" Although it seemed a shame to miss this phenomenal movie scene, I had been amply indoctrinated to follow the orders of my superiors. After all, not knowing it, I would become a not-so-salty gunnery sergeant in the not too distant future. So, below deck I went. The looks I received from my fit-for-battle fellow grunts spelled total disbelief that anyone could be so naïve.

To cover my embarrassment, I explained my behavior with a swagger and wondered why everyone else had been so chicken. Swagger is what my comrades had taught me since reporting in to Camp Le Jeune. I knew that they saw right through my bluster, and so I sheepishly faded into the background, hoping that our attention could be turned to something more important.

As we waited to disembark, it was getting late and, for me, it had been a pretty exciting day. I thought it would be a good idea to find some place to rest. Waiting can be boring. So, I found a secluded corner below and curled up for a brief shut-eye. It must have been longer than I thought, for when I awakened, the Marines had landed. Most of them. The landing at Inchon had to be perfectly timed to coincide with the ebb and flow of the tides. Once the troops and equipment were ashore, the LCVP had to resituate itself back into the bay before the tide receded. So, there was this one young, dumb Marine aboard the otherwise empty ship, along with the ship's company, with no clue as to what the next move would be. My rifle, along with the rest of my gear, had been taken ashore with the other equipment. I now found myself face-to-face with my newly acquired sailor friends who were as bewildered as I. Finally, someone made the decision to get me ashore, ostensibly to rejoin me with my unit.

I was put aboard an M-boat (LCM–Landing Craft Mechanized), which is a smaller craft carried aboard the larger landing ship (LCVP–Vehicle/Personnel). Today I would do virtually anything to have a video or transcript of this lone, idiotic, clueless nineteen-year-old making his own unarmed landing at Inchon. I see myself as MacArthur wading ashore victoriously at Tacloban in the Philippines. A major difference, though, is that I was not accompanied by hundreds of troops in the background to back me up. In fact, I was alone, a private first class, with nothing but the promise of trouble ahead, regardless of the outcome of this particular venture. I was making my personal Inchon Landing.

The assault landing targeted three beaches: Red, Green, and Blue. The Fifth Marines were to land at Red and Green Beaches, while our own First Marines were to enter at Blue Beach, which was some distance from the other two. My sailor friends dropped me off in what I thought to be No-Man's-Land, but what really turned out to be Blue Beach. Apparently the First Marines had already taken this route, for there was ample devastating evidence. First of all, I had absolutely no idea as to the whereabouts of my unit, the First Combat Service Group. As I strolled leisurely down roads already traveled by our troops, I felt like Huckleberry Finn, (without his friend, Big Jim), unarmed, except for a branch that I used to poke at things I encountered along the way. Here I was on Korean soil. Even the most frivolous things were no different from what I was accustomed to seeing: ruts in the road, the trees and other vegetation, birds that, though rare, seemed not to be different from the ones back home. What *was* different was the stilled bodies of Koreans along the road, some of which had been done in by gunfire and flame-throwers. Suddenly, things began to become real to me. This was no longer maneuvers. The players, such as those lying in ditches along the road, would not simply clean up afterwards and settle down for the evening. I could not playfully poke them with my Huck Finn branch to awaken them from their make-believe deaths. This was no longer "Bang! You're dead," like the games I played as a child not so long ago.

The transition from boy to man would begin to take shape during that stroll. But this was only the beginning of the transition. It would take significantly more incidents and time to make me understand the seriousness of where I was and what I was doing. Something bigger and wiser than I somehow guided me to my outfit, for I was wandering aimlessly along the countryside. I could just as easily have headed in the opposite direction, into the hands or, worse, the sights of the enemy. I was understandably relieved to see the familiar faces of our bedraggled group. Once again, I was overcome with embarrassment. And once again, I was greeted with disgust. William, my best friend from childhood, was distraught, believing that I had maybe not survived the landing. Through tears, he gave me the "what for," which made me feel really guilty, more for having put him through such an ordeal than for my own safety and stupidity. William was not the only one just a bit more than upset. Our all-Black unit was led by a young, redheaded white second lieutenant, who promised me that when we got settled, he would bring me up on charges. That never happened, and I always wondered why not. Was it because there were many other more important things to be concerned about? Was it because I was young and stupid? I came to appreciate why I was spared a bit later on as my career became marked by fits and starts. Fortunately, there were more starts than fits.

As I review the major turning points in my life, high on the list would be that Inchon Landing and its aftermath. It was the first time I would view the value of life critically. The exposure to the dead bodies of enemy troops was one thing, even the beginning of a wake-up call. But the real epiphany emerged on the morning of September 16, 1950, the day after the invasion. That is the day that reality hit me right between the eyes. In surveying the damage wrought by the assault, I saw as many dead bodies of Marines as the eye can process, although I learned that the "fewer than three hundred" that we suffered were fewer than expected. Many of the faces that I saw were familiar to me. Some I had joked with just a few days before. Some I knew from back in the States. Now, they were lying here covered with their own ponchos, some with their dog tags stuck between their dry teeth. It was here that I began to question what warfare was all about. Obviously, groups necessarily have to defend themselves, or they will not long survive. But when I am reminded that a certain number of casualties are calculated in a military campaign, while certainly rational, I am presented with moral questions that, for me, have yet to be sufficiently answered. Though it may be expected that losses will occur, one can only use numbers in the equation, not names. It's a crapshoot. We know that a percentage of us will die, but we cannot say which ones.

Maybe this is a naïve perspective because, after all, isn't this what life is about? The carnage of the highways, famines, diseases, violence in the streets? My problem is reconciling our obsession, on the one hand, with the preservation of human life while, on the other hand, to continually seek ways to more efficiently destroy humankind. After all, efficient warfare is about taking as many enemy lives as possible, in the shortest possible time, with the fewest casualties on your side. Is man, by nature, antagonistic, even without survival issues to pit one group against another? If not, then why is it that in almost all cultures analysts are at the drawing boards or in labs figuring ways to kill more people more efficiently, in terms of numbers and time? Is this what civility is about?

I always cringe when governmental leaders, news reporters, military leaders, political parties, and even rank and file citizens quote casualty numbers as

though they do not involve people. I always look at casualty figures expo-
nentially, thinking in terms of how many lives are touched by the loss of
one person. It certainly doesn't add up to "fewer than three hundred." At
this writing, there have been more than 4,100 U.S. deaths in Iraq, as well
as approximately 17,000 wounded. It would be interesting to follow the life
of any one of these young men and women to see how many others are
impacted by the loss.

I continue to notice that those who take casualty figures lightly are those
who, too often, have never been in harm's way, have never seen death up
close, and too often have used institutional means to avoid the hazards of
war. Very often, these are the people who make up the ranks of the "Hawks."
It is not unusual for the reality of death in warfare to make believers of
combatants. Another cause for indifference on the part of the privileged is
the inordinate number of people who go into the armed forces for economic
reasons. Many who enlist have no other legitimate options. My own several
attempts at the military option (the Air Force, and finally the Marines) were
due, primarily, to the lack of attainable or acceptable civilian work. The romantic ideal and the childhood quest for adventure were secondary reasons
for those decisions. The consequence was that I found myself in league with
almost a complete cadre of young men who were in the same boat as I. It
was the only escape hatch available to the majority of us from the downward
spiral of hopelessness, crime, and poverty.

The Korean Conflict has been called an "undeclared war," a "brushfire,"
"The Forgotten War," none of which rang true for even the most unsophisticated of those of us who were there. At least in retrospect, for although
there was obviously a grand scheme afoot far above our heads, our personal
reasons for being there were not primarily about patriotism but mostly about
happenstance.

And so, with the landing completed, it was now time to get established by
setting up a bivouac area reminiscent of the television show *MASH*. This
is where we would remain until the next operation—which meant North
Korea. One of the first things the younger ones of us would install was a
makeshift basketball court. Shows where our priorities were. It was like a
small community, with a mess hall, a sick-bay, a brig-tent, areas for doing
laundry, administrative offices, and, of course, housing tents—three men per
tent. All of the normal bivouac routines were maintained, including security
measures, e.g., sentry duties. This amounted to a formula for disaster for me,
for I still hadn't gotten it, regarding the level of seriousness of this grown-up

game that we were now playing. So now I got assigned to sentry duty. My tour begins at midnight.

It so happens that the preceding day had been an exceptionally hectic one: a demanding work schedule, a hard afternoon shooting hoops at the make-shift basket-on-a-pole, an early evening spent washing and hanging my personal laundry. I went on guard duty at midnight absolutely exhausted, so it did not take very long for me to succumb to the temptation to take a brief nap. After all, things were safe enough here in our neighborhood, and wasn't guard duty simply a silly way to harass the troops? Guess again. This was a war zone, and danger was ever present. And here I was asleep. The whole free-world relying on me for its safety, to protect democracy, liberty, freedom of choice, petroleum products (wherever they may be), and our particular ethnocentric way of defining "right" and "wrong." Forget the ideological concerns. I was caught sleeping at the most inopportune time and place. The Uniform Code of Military Justice (UCMJ) reads:

913. Article 113–Misbehavior of a Sentinel or Lookout

Any sentinel or lookout who is found drunk or sleeping upon his post, or leaves it before regularly relieved, shall be punished, if the offense is committed in time of war, by death or such punishment as a court-martial may direct, if the offense is committed at any other time, by such punishment as court-martial may direct.

In spite of the grammatical structure, the message is very clear: You go to sleep on post in wartime and you are subject to possible execution. Pretty serious business. But I did not receive a death sentence and was not knowledgeable enough to be aware of the possibilities. The levels of disciplinary actions ranked, in order of severity, from unit commander's discretion to summary court martial, to special court martial, to general court martial. I was brought up before the unit commander for office hours, found guilty, and sentenced to ten days in the makeshift brig. The experience did very little to impress upon me the gravity of the situation, for the "brig" turned out to be one of the many tents where we bivouacked with very little security, and with a sentry who tended to look the other way as my friends sneaked cigarettes, beer, and other goodies under the sides of the tent. I've always wondered why I was treated so liberally by the unit commander, and

William and me in Kobe, Japan.

to this day can only speculate as to the rationale. Looking back, I feel that I was extremely fortunate, whatever the rationale. It could have been that, in the total scheme of things, my situation was small potatoes. There was a war to be fought. Or maybe it was their perception of this pitiful, naïve, young private first class who probably had marbles and a rabbit's foot in his pocket. Or maybe it was because, aside from a couple of lapses in responsibility, I really was a pretty good Marine, as the future would discover. In spite of a basic tenet in the military ranks that one never volunteers for anything, I volunteered for everything, a lesson that I learned from my otherwise irresponsible stepfather. My friend William was just the opposite. He had better skills at getting out of tasks than meeting them head-on. While his tendency might have seemed appropriate (and actually cool) to most of the troops, I feel certain that it didn't serve him well over the long term, for he acquired a label that would not go away. I always felt that he was far more talented and insightful than I. The curious upshot of the punishment experience was that the morning immediately after returning to my unit, a company formation was routinely called, and I heard my name called. "Pfc. John West, front and center!" I thought, "Christ, what did I do now?" Apparently the signals got mixed, for instead of being further embarrassed, I was promoted to corporal—by the same unit commander who had given me brig time. This was my first exposure to the absurdity of bureaucracies. In those days, in the Marine Corps, being corporal was a big deal, for it meant having control and responsibility that was totally alien to me, and for the moment I was not prepared to be "A leader of men." I did manage to warm to the task in pretty short order, though I felt pangs of guilt because William was not promoted. Since childhood, we'd always done everything together.

We, William and I, have always had a lot in common: the coming of age, both being married far too early, both having been inordinately influenced by parents (in his case his grandparents who were his custodians), both now receiving negative feedback from sources in Birmingham about our errant young wives at home. (I do believe that William never completely recovered from the rumors, and I often wonder why I survived.) My immediate reaction was to get out of the relationship, an infeasible notion on my part, being thousands of miles from home. I asked my mother to begin some sort of proceedings on my behalf, with power-of-attorney, so as to put an end to what had been a totally traumatic experience from the moment of her pregnancy. Mama refused. I'll never know why, but I suspected that she was perhaps sensitive to the situation from a woman's perspective. As we will see later, that refusal may have been the precursor to a number of tragic outcomes. It didn't help that what was projected to be a three-month stint in Korea would turn out to be a year and three months. So, it was a matter of either making a psychological adjustment to the situation or going off the rails. I thought that I was in control and could make the necessary adjustments and would deal with it all later. Wrong.

By the time of the Inchon Landing, war had been raging in Korea for almost four months. And it had not gone smoothly. The landing offered promise of better fortunes. By late September, Seoul, the South Korea capitol, had been taken by our troops. Things were looking good. In the ranks, men were once again beginning to believe that the end was in sight. That is when the worse period of the war began for our side. Moving north, we crossed the mythical 38th Parallel. Almost simultaneously, Chinese communists came across the Yalu River from China in overwhelming numbers such that no amount of technology or military expertise could possibly withstand the onslaught. It was out of this situation that the greatest amount of tragedy and heroism was manifested. Marines were eventually surrounded by the Chinese and North Koreans. When Marine Colonel Lewis "Chesty" Puller was asked what his next move would be, he is reported to have responded with bluster, "They're on our left flank, our right flank, in the rear of us, in front of us. They won't get away this time!" Another undocumented Puller quote was,

"At least we'll know where they (the enemy) will be in the morning. That's more than we can say about the Army." Marines hate the Army.

The North Koreans and Chinese were responsible for the now notorious "Death March," which lost over one hundred POW's and civilians to murder by their captors. The "March" covered one hundred miles in cold, freezing, and rainy weather. Following that tragedy, came the "Trap" at the Chosin Reservoir, which was equally tragic, not only for the loss of lives and horrible frostbite injuries, but also the huge blow to tradition and pride of the Marine Corps. We were beaten, primarily by the sheer numbers the enemy threw at us. It has become clear to me, because of the numbers of set-backs or near-misses we have suffered militarily since WWI, that a large part of our problem is that we wind up fighting forces that we choose not to understand—until it is too late, at which point we scurry around and try to figure it out. I am also convinced that this is due, to too great an extent, to our arrogance born of privilege. It happened in World War II, when we had no clue as to the mentality of the Japanese at war. We saw them stereotypically as a passive, non-violent people who were so kind that warfare was not conducive to their national personality. Maybe we should have taken the time to review their history. Maybe then we could have understood kamikaze raids, banzai attacks, and the resort to hari-kari (self-disembowelment) in the event of failure. The very nature of our culture is not conducive to altruistic suicide.

And then we did it again with regards to Korea. How were we to guess that masses of screaming, horn-blowing Chinese would pour across the Yalu River with such abandonment that there seemed to be little regard for their own personal lives? Could it happen again in such places as Afghanistan and Iraq? Would it be beneficial to have some appreciation of one's enemy's psyche to anticipate reactions and tendencies? For some cultures, the cause is more important than life itself.

My own record from the Korean War reads like this: "Participated in the assault and seizure of Inchon, Korea; the capture and securing of Seoul, Korea; the Wonsan-Hungnam-Chosin Campaign, Northern Korea; Operations against enemy forces in South and Central Korea 15 Aug. 50 - 27 Nov. 51, Korea." The citations that I received include The Korean Service Medal with Five Battle Stars, The United Nations Service Medal, The Army of Occupation (Japan), The Korean Defense Commemorative Medal, The National Defense Service Medal, The Presidential Unit Citation, and The Korean Presidential Unit Citation. If we overlook sleeping through the Inchon Landing and a later little nap while on guard duty, the rest of my

William and me in North Korea.

involvement was not too bad. I think that eventually I learned that this was not the venue in which to relax. The *blue skies* part of all of this is that today I cannot go to sleep any time or place not designated for such. I awaken at the drop of a feather. I am an extremely early riser. And I am enthralled with teaching time management and all that it entails. So, once you get past not being executed for sleeping on post, the rest is easy.

Somehow, we managed to get out of the mess that some blamed General Douglas MacArthur for getting us into. We boarded sea craft that had come to rescue us and headed all the way back down to the Pusan Perimeter, almost the southernmost end of Korea. After all the negotiations at high levels, the 38th Parallel was established with the demilitarized zone, symbolic of a war not won and of a divided people, similar to what happened with regards to East and West Germany and North and South Vietnam. The *blue skies* for me, personally, were that I, unlike many of my more skillful and sophisticated comrades, emerged from this debacle unscathed, but with tons of experience that would serve as a foundation for a lifetime of development, which is still unfolding after three-quarters of a century.

On November 27, 1951, fifteen months after we embarked on our "three-month" expedition, we were on a ship headed back to the States (me, with my new front teeth, acquired in Japan). We docked at Broadway Pier in San Diego to the welcome of hundreds of well-wishers and family members. William and I expected no one, and, of course, there was no one. We promptly boarded a train (Only the affluent traveled by air back then.) and headed to Birmingham for a 30-day leave. I was met at the train station by my father, who, thinking it was the right thing to do, brought along Juliet, for he was unaware of the nature of my relationship with her. I will always ponder the significance of that fateful meeting with her. I did not want to get re-involved with someone that I would never trust again. But fate, family interaction, and Ronnie, our only son at that juncture, found me slowly warming to the possibility of a positive future. Wrong. Herein lays the danger of a lack of total resolve. This is a decision I will always regret at the most basic level. In the aftermath of that decision, I have grown resolute, giving the most important issues the most thorough consideration before making a decision, but once the decision is made, my resolve is to never look back. That is where I went wrong in December 1951, upon returning home. I second-guessed myself. Where were the *blue skies*? Sometimes they come later. Much later.

15

SAN FRANCISCO

My next assignment, coming out of Korea, was MCDA, San Francisco. How on earth did I wind up at one of the most desired duty stations in the Marine Corps? Beautiful downtown San Francisco! With its stage shows along Market Street, unbelievable food everywhere, the Filmore District with its great jazz clubs and eateries, Golden Gate Park, and the Marine Corps Office building at the foot of the Bay Bridge, where I worked. It was then and there that I established that there was no city in the world that I would ever compare with San Francisco.

Towards getting things somewhat normal with Juliet, I proposed that I would get military family housing and that she could join me in San Francisco when it was done. Very frankly, I expected some resistance on her mother's part, but proceeded with things as planned. The housing came through, and my wife and son soon arrived at the train station in San Francisco, and for the first time ever we were together, alone, with what was to be without any outside influence. Things were looking up. I thought.

For a time, we relied solely on public transportation to get around the city. Surprisingly, it was fun and adventuresome. It is actually better not to have a car in San Francisco, a painful lesson I would learn later. I carpooled downtown to work with another Marine who lived nearby. But soon it seemed appropriate to reciprocate. I needed a car. The first problem was that I had no experience driving in city traffic. In fact, I had no driver's license. But I had received a lump sum of money for combat pay and saw no reason why I should not use it to purchase a car. So, I began to shop along automobile row on Van Ness until I found something that fascinated me: a 1949 Ford two-door coupe that was faster than a speeding bullet. Perfect for someone who didn't know how to drive. In the congested Van Ness area, some of the auto dealerships were situated on multiple floors. This particular one used spiral driveways from top to bottom. At this point, my driving had been restricted to jeeps and pick-up trucks in open fields in Korea. No license necessary in Korea. Hence, I was handed the keys to a stick shift hot little car on the third floor and was expected to drive off smoothly, down the ramp, up Mission Street, and to home. I managed to get down the ramp to the street with embarrassing jerks (I was in first gear) and then on my way up Mission Street, several miles from downtown, to Geneva Avenue. All in first gear. The gearshifts on jeeps had been on the floor.

Now the stage was set for my disastrous driving experiences in downtown San Francisco, with its hills and cable cars. It seemed that there was at the very least a fender-bender each week. I was dangerous. I had absolutely no feel whatsoever for the concept of lane changes. Driving in San Francisco is a challenge for the most experienced drivers. I, as a novice, was like a ball in a pinball machine among them. Another of the many close calls that I would somehow survive.

On March 29, 1953, our second son, John, Jr., was born in San Francisco. We were now four and began to look more and more like a real family, although there still remained some feelings of trepidation on my part and maybe some buyer's remorse on her part. But we muddled through and I got into that ambivalent mode, as I am wont to do, which claims that regardless to the hopelessness of situations, if one puts one's nose to the grindstone and keeps working, one will ultimately prevail. I would have plenty of opportunities to test that theory in the years to come. Sometimes, even in the direst of circumstances, some extraordinarily wonderful things are possible. John, Jr., was the epitome of *blue skies*.

Other good things happened for me in San Francisco. On March 1, 1952, at age twenty, I was promoted to sergeant. At least this time, it felt earned. By this time I was doing clerical work in the administrative offices. After some time, being bored, I decided to brush the dust off my musical skills and auditioned for the Marine Corps Band at the Naval Air Station, Treasure Island. I was accepted and got my first taste of life as a full-time professional musician, a role that is played out twenty-four hours a day, seven days a week. There was no particular genre or specialty. The band played symphonic concerts, jazz performances on television's KRON, San Francisco, and parades/concerts at Sacramento's State Fair, in Reno, in Vallejo, and other points north. This would be the first of three Marine Bands with which I would eventually perform.

San Francisco was the first truly cosmopolitan city that I was totally immersed in. I learned to avoid confusing familiarity with tolerance. I liked the idea of a hodge-podge of cultures co-existing in a congested, land-locked Mediterranean-like city. At first glance, it would appear that the co-existence was peaceful, certainly more so than I had known. However, upon closer examination, one would find all sorts of divisions based more on ethnicity than race, though race was, indeed, a factor. San Francisco continues to be influenced politically and culturally by Chinese-Americans, Italian-Americans, and to a lesser extent, Blacks and Latinos (each at about 6.5 percent). Italian-Americans are included in the white category, which comprises forty-three percent of the total population. With my now guarded optimism, I observed a new level of acceptance of the differences that inevitably existed among us. It was not unusual to perceive several different languages being spoken all around me, although I did not understand any of them, except a reasonable bit of Japanese and, a little bit of Korean, and some high school Spanish. It seemed enriching, mainly because no one seemed intimidated by alien sounds. I have, on the other hand, in other parts of California, especially Southern California, witnessed people being offended if someone spoke a foreign language in their presence. "Why don't they speak American?" "What've they got to hide?" "They must be talking about me."

There seemed to be a symbiotic relationship between Chinese-Americans and African-Americans. One notices that, when in the same boat, accommodation for paddling in the same direction becomes necessary for survival. Failing to figure out that necessity has proven to be disastrous where population succession has meant serious contention. There is a level of political sophistication in the Bay Area that appears to be absent in many other parts of the state. This is only one of the many fascinations I have with San Francisco. Having traveled with the Marine Corps band to most of the major cities in this country, "The City," with its moles and pock marks, is hands-down my absolute favorite. I promised myself that I'd spend the final days of my life there, only to be sidetracked by unforeseen circumstances: perfect year-round tennis weather in what I perceive to be less culturally sophisticated Southern California and, most importantly, involvement with my extended family, including my children and my many grand- and great grandchildren. I do have priorties.

16

BARSTOW AND
POINTS SOUTH

I struggle, as I look back, to find rationale for my requesting a transfer from San Francisco after a spell. Restlessness? What is more puzzling is to request Barstow, California. Barstow—a hellhole in the desert. Nebo, Daggett, Yermo. Housing was a trailer. There was absolutely nothing to do except for a few on-base activities, no place to go. For the first two months, before acquiring base housing, my family roomed with a kind lady in San Bernardino. I drove the 150-mile roundtrip to and from Barstow each day. My fast little Ford earned me a speeding citation in Victorville. There was no freeway; there was only Route 66, which was a series of sand dunes. However, I was able to squeeze a little over one hundred miles per hour out of Betsy, and it cost me dearly.

One of my duties was to serve as Sgt. of the Guard at Yermo. This entailed checking posts at all hours. Irony of ironies! I was to ensure that sentries were alert, not goofing off, and, of course, not sleeping while on duty. I would cringe, hoping that I would not have to re-live my transgressions through others. Fortunately, it never came to that. Apparently, they were more conscientious than I had been. Or perhaps my timing was off, or theirs was better.

Barstow was enough to make even a seasoned traveler, like me, homesick. And so, when I had the opportunity to re-enlist, it certainly was not to extend my stay there. I requested to be transferred to Albany, Georgia, which was the closest I could get to Birmingham. This meant that I would be able to visit my folks often, as the distance through Columbus, Georgia, was only about a hundred miles or so. But before we would depart for Georgia, I had this wonderful idea of going back to Los Angeles to have my hot little Ford re-painted by shops that advertised a complete paint job in one day for $19.95. So we backtracked to Los Angeles, visited with some aunts, uncles, and cousins as the car was being painted. Why I chose powder blue, I'll never know.

Finally, we were off to points southeast, via route 66. It had been warm in California, and I had no reason to suspect that it would be any different driving across country. Things were progressing pretty smoothly until we got into Arizona. There was a drastic change in climate, and suddenly I was confronted with elements that were totally unexpected. It was freezing, and the roads were slick. I had only recently gotten accustomed to driving under normal conditions. Oh, I could drive fast, but caution and safety were different issues. Now I was moving along at the posted speed limit, which was too fast for existing road conditions. Just up ahead of me, on this two-lane road, was a stalled flatbed truck. I saw it in what seemed to be plenty of time, but inexperience took over, and as I applied the brakes gingerly, we were approaching the truck in very slow motion, with a feeling of unbelievable helplessness. Even the resulting impact, though tenuous, was enough to totally disable the car. It's the last I ever saw of the newly painted Betsy. My inexperience ill prepared me to deal with such matters. I had no idea what my rights were. I think that because of my lack of sophistication, I was taken advantage of by my insurance company. We wound up having to get a motel in Holbrook, Arizona and made arrangements to get the next train to Birmingham, sans Betsey.

17

ALBANY, GA
(AL-BEENY)

After a few days at home, it was time to report to my next duty station at Marine Corps Depot of Supplies, Albany, Georgia. I went on alone to explore the possibilities of housing. A cousin in Birmingham informed me that we had distant relatives in Albany, and that they would be a good source of, if nothing else, information. I stayed with them for a short time, was directed to an acquaintance of theirs and found a nice place to rent near the downtown area. After a few months there, we learned that a new housing tract was being built on the other side of town and that we could be eligible to purchase one of the homes. The possibility seemed remote to me, for the purchase price for a new, two-bedroom home was $5,000. The quality of the homes was nothing to brag about, but they were new, clean, and located in a nice area. It was all kind of exciting for me, as a new first-time homeowner. I began to make essential improvements immediately, e.g., a basketball goal in the backyard. And also some not-so-essential additions, such as the posts-and-rope fencing around the front yard. My engineering skills had not taken into consideration that when it rained, the cute little rope lines would shrink and become taut, which was a source of deep consternation for me. I also called upon my neglected carpentry skills to build lawn furniture, for which I was rather proud. If asked at any point in my young life what I'd most like to become, it would have been, without question, a carpenter—a close-tolerance cabinetmaker. Though I love teaching more than anything else I've ever done, there are instances in the bureaucracy of it all when carpentry is the high ground. Carpentry is kind, forgiving (if you're willing to tear down something that is imperfect and start all over), and keeps the creative juices flowing continually, even after completion of a satisfying product.

My neighbors, as well as the civilians that I worked with on base, gave me ample opportunity to get in touch with African-American culture in Albany. This was the first community in my military assignments in which I would become thoroughly immersed. I got to know and appreciate families, community dynamics, political issues (and they were significant), and the core values that drove and sustained the day-to-day lives of a very segregated community.

Albany, because of Albany State University (formerly "State College"—it seems that there are few four-year "colleges" anymore), and Albany Technical College, is essentially a college town. This accounts, in large part, for African-Americans being unwilling to settle for the injustices that have pervaded the city historically. It was the site of much racial unrest, which had grown considerably due to civil rights activities throughout the country. Many of my acquaintances had either attended or graduated from what was then Albany State College. My associations with them were the continuation of the attraction to education that had dogged me overseas. It was, once again, the long arm of Mama's influence, that imposing sheepskin from Spelman College that always graced our walls wherever we lived.

In Korea, I had fantasized about getting into somebody's college, as I had foolishly done about attending Tuskegee Institute to become a veterinarian while doing horribly in the sciences in high school. I relished the possibility of returning to the states, getting out of the Marine Corps, and attending Compton College, the community college for which I had my only college catalog, which I read every night. I was prepared to do anything. I would be willing to work at the college as a custodian or a groundskeeper, or whatever was necessary, just to be in the environment while taking courses.

It is probable that nothing preoccupied me more while in the Marines than the nagging notion that I should be in school. Some of my experiences with people in higher positions, but with less intelligence, continued to remind me that factors such as racism and not having the necessary credentials or paperwork put me at a disadvantage. In the back of my mind, I knew where those conditions would eventually take me. As the saying goes, "My Mama didn't raise no fools." And although the credentialing, which can sometimes amount to nonsense, can be effectively overcome, racism is still a major factor in practically all decision-making in this society. Even as I write, Barack Obama holds a significant lead over his opponent, John McCain, for the November 4 election. It will be interesting to note the impact of racism in this election, even among those who are currently inclined to vote democratic. Some of the pundits have insisted that race will, indeed, become a factor for some when ballots are actually cast, which, at this point, should be a non-issue. I do, however, believe that regardless of the outcome, much will have been done to help eradicate racism in this country as we have known it. I also doubt that voters who choose not to cast their votes for Barack Obama will have a significant impact on what I think will be his victory—the country's victory.

Albany State University is a historically black college, its influence felt strongly in the Black community in Albany. The Black community was at once an educated community and one that spoke openly and often of its superstitions. The power of "Goober Dust," when used judiciously, could have profound impact on an adversary. The dreadful curse of having someone threatening to "pray on you" could produce extremely negative effects. Nothing scientific, but if the belief permeates the culture, it might as well be true. It was, however, difficult to discern where the line was drawn between the believers and the non-believers. I, as an observer, felt both comfortable with and fascinated by it all.

The Marine Corps base in Albany was relatively new, so that Marines were a novelty to the community. The command began to think in terms of PR with the community. What better way, other than providing civil service jobs, to get the attention of the public than to establish a Marine Corps Band. This was a band built from scratch, garnering the talents of existing staff, former bandsmen, new people who had musical backgrounds, and a few who were transferred in for the purpose. So, off I go into a fledgling unit with no place to go but up. But up it went. And soon we were, as with San Francisco, traveling around the southeastern part of the country doing what Marine Bands do. In addition, we did a lot of local dance work, and an off-shoot of that was a group that I formed, which played local clubs, including VFW establishments out in the woods and the one small Black club in the center of the community. One of the issues that never occurred to me and never caused a problem was the racial make-up of my combo. The members came from the band on the base, which was obviously integrated and so was the combo. I like to think that we were an entertaining group, much appreciated by our audiences, without consideration for our racial makeup.

The assignment to Albany gave me ample opportunity to make frequent short trips to Birmingham to satisfy my need to cure homesickness. But some other opportunities came out of it for Juliet, my errant wife. Being the slow learner, it took me literally years to figure out that Birmingham was, and had been while I was abroad, her "briar patch," to take a term from *Brer Rabbit*, who claimed to dread being thrown into the briar patch. But at being thrown in, he said, "Born and bred in the briar patch, Brer Fox," and happily skipped off. He only feigned fear. It was where he desperately wanted to be all along. Her opportunities had abounded for the fifteen months while I was away. Her rah-rah activities with the Miles College Band and cheer squad and time spent in Birmingham as I was making duty station changes were windows of opportunity that never remotely occurred to me. Many of the negatives that I now allude to came out in her therapy sessions in a crisis mental state much later. I learned far more than I wanted to know.

Albany was another of her many "opportunities." A male neighbor, who lived next door to our neat little tract home, was one who feigned some kind of emotional incapacity. He was a postal employee on disability and around home all day, as his teacher wife worked. He and Juliet spent far too much time commiserating, a situation which caused on-going conflict in our home. Although this was indicative of a larger, more established pattern, I now shudder to think of the depths of my denial at that point.

I am a hopeless romantic. But my style of love goes beyond Eros, or storge, or mania. It includes a deep love of history, of things or relationships of the past. I am continually attempting to reconnect with old friends and places. I am not one who sees the past simply as the past, but as the foundation for all things that follow. So, it figures that I would try to resurrect all of the many relationships from boot camp, to Korea, to my civilian friends from San Francisco and Georgia, and to the Marines that I shared good and bad times with. So, what have I learned in my many attempts to reconnect? That too many of them have died, that some of them hardly remember the connections, and so what I discover is not always very pleasant. I recently called information and got the numbers of a couple of fairly close friends I had known in Albany. After reaching one person using the name I remembered, I was disappointed that he seemed vague and had what seemed to be a difficult time recalling our acquaintance. It turned out that I'd reached the "Junior" of my friend, Elijah Richardson, and that my friend had died some years earlier. A similar situation occurred with another "Junior" in Albany, Edgar Martin, Jr. Ah, the names that almost seem ghost-like today: "Chick" Washington, Elijah Richardson, Carrie and Edgar Martin, and Edgar, Jr., who when asked as a child by a Sunday school teacher to request a song for the class to sing, inquired, innocently, "Do y'all know "Hearts made of stone, doody wa, doody wa, will never break, doody wa, doody wa?" These losses indicated to me, once again, that you really couldn't go home again. But home in this instance is called "Al-beeny," not "Al'bany."

Albany produced my fourth promotion, this time to staff sergeant, as well as our third son Gerald. With the promotion came new responsibilities and privileges, along with swagger sticks and staff NCO clubs. I got the feeling that all of this was being thrust upon me without preparation and that it was necessary, once again, to get up to speed in a hurry. I was beginning to feel like a very responsible young adult—because I had no other choice.

While stationed at Albany, I was sent to the U.S. Army Transportation School at Fort Eustis, Newport News, Virginia. It was the most effective school I would attend in the military, and I would attend many. The instructors were top-notch and made me begin to think in terms of what effective instruction is all about. There is nothing that I did not learn about every aspect of every mode of transportation in this country and the Department of Transportation's role in regulating it. The assignment also gave me my first glimpse of places like Williamsburg and Jamestown, Virginia. But, more importantly, it gave me the opportunity to visit my Uncle Skeet (Mama's brother) and his family in Charlottesville. It so happened that my mother was visiting the family at the same time, so it was a nice, though brief, reunion. Here, I met five cousins: Thomasine, Howard, Ronnie, Vernetta, and Brenda, whose numbers have been decimated by sixty percent. Only Vernetta and Thomasine remain. Because the deceased were all considerably younger than I, their deaths seem appropriately untimely to me. I remain very close to Vernetta and her family. (See cp-12. #1).

While at Fort Eustis, I also met an old acquaintance from Camp Le Jeune, James "Jake" Hollins. Hollins and I would serve together in two other venues in the fifties: Marine Corps Air Station at Cherry Point, North Carolina, and Naval Air Station, Edenton, North Carolina.

Mama,
circa 1942.

My wife, Suzanne,
who gave me a new
lease on life and
is a totally dedi-
cated mother and
grandmother.

Birmingham Civil Rights Institute, lest we forget.

A small, cleaned up industrial area where 222 So. 13th Street used to be.

"Munga," the horrible swimming hole, complete with human excrement.

Titusville and Golden Flake.

The A&P, once a supermarket / warehouse, where I got into my first potentially serious trouble with the bar of Ivory soap and where I scavenged and played among dangerous railway sidings.

Kress 5 & 10 cents store where I shopped for Mama, but also where I illegally procured little rubber cars.

Hillman Hospital, my birthplace, currently a part of UAB Medical Center.

Westminster Presbyterian Church, where John Rice, Condoleezza's grandfather, pastored when Bay-Suh and I were required to attend.

Bay-Suh and me for her 70th birthday at her home in Las Vegas.

13

*The old "48" house number that I made in woodshop at Ullman High, in 1946,
which I removed in 2000, replacing it with . . .*

14

The new "48," which I constructed with tile and oak frame.

"The Corner," where I hung out listening to the lies and conquests of older boys.

Ullman Junior High School, now swallowed up by University of Alabama.

*The Principal's Office where
I spent major amounts of time
waiting to be chastised by
Mr. George Bell.*

*The old Parker High School with its wonderful architecture, a source of pride
for all who passed through its portals.*

19

The new Parker High School architecture, a disappointment to us old-timers.

20

Bay-Suh revisiting Tuxedo Junction.

"The House," rooms for rent. $2 per hour, where Juliet and I had our lives temporarily defined.

Smithfield Projects, which felt rather upscale for government housing. No Riff-Raff allowed.

My cousin Vernetta and me.

Loveman Village, projects where Juliet's mother lived. Where I made the mistake of falling ill.

Red clay road in West Point, Georgia etched in a child's memory.

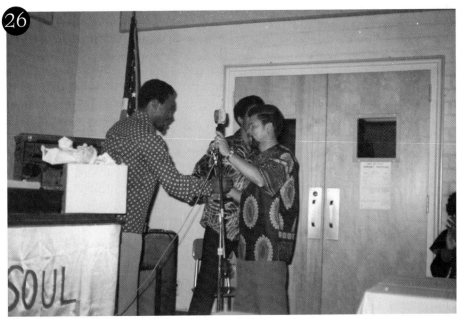

A Black Student's Union function at Santa Ana College, dashiki days.

Bubba and his wife, Gloria, at Parker's class of '49 fiftieth reunion.

Classmate, Charles Brown, and popular teacher, Ms. Helen George, at Parker's fiftieth '49er reunion.

29

Grandpa reading to Shea, granddaughter, and Brianna, great granddaughter.

30

My kids, sans Josh.

My son Josh and his wife Sarah.

Family at Christmastime, on the occasion of the 100 Black Men's Gala.

The "wealthy steps" of cousins Harrison and Jean McKinney.

Our "poor steps" at 48 4th Avenue South (now razed).

Birmingham Jail, where Dr. King wrote his "Letter from Birmingham Jail."

Woodshop at Ullman High School where I made #48 house number.
Now Anthropology Forensics lab at UAB.

Sculpture of Police Dogs used by "Bull" Connor. Kelly Ingram Park.

Sculpture of water cannons used by "Bull" Connor. Kelly Ingram Park.

39

Home in Mission Viejo, California.

18

CHERRY POINT
AND EDENTON, NC

I was next transferred to Marine Corps Air Station, Cherry Point, North Carolina. I renewed acquaintance with Hollins, a fellow traveler from Camp Le Jeune and Korea. We would find our careers paralleling for the next two assignments, working literally side by side and living with our families in the same communities. I would begin to view him as my new "best friend," for I had long since lost contact with William. But I learned, without trying, that those earlier ties cannot be expunged with distance, and William would always be there.

Cherry Point was an interesting place, for although it was the principle entity in the little town outside the air station gate, aside from local economics, it didn't seem to wield too much influence in Havelock, N. C., the local town. Black Marine families in the community had to ship their children off on school buses nineteen or twenty miles to New Bern to attend school. On many occasions the buses would break down, and parents would either have to retrieve their children or allow them to arrive to school very late. In the meantime, there was a public school situated in the middle of the base-housing complex where we lived. But it was called a "white" school. I, and a few other families, could not believe the absurdity of the arrangement and confronted the school system, which eventually capitulated and moved into the twentieth century.

The housing was the very best we had experienced. It was spacious and well maintained. We did have an incident in which one of the wall heaters had its flues become obstructed, and we barely awoke the next morning due to near asphyxiation by carbon monoxide. The *blue skies* were that we did wake up. In fact, it was here that our fourth son, Reggie, was born. It amazes me that so many children can be born to horrible relationships. There are few things more dangerous than denial. And do the children suffer as a result of being born into such conditions? Time would tell.

The band at Cherry Point gave me my best view of this country. We seemed to be constantly traveling. (See page # 109). A memorable excursion involved the opening of the Saint Lawrence Seaway, begun in 1954 to link the Great Lakes to the Atlantic Ocean. The band played marathon engagements from Sandusky and Cleveland, Ohio, to Buffalo, New York. The performances involved massive parades and periodic concerts in town centers. We traveled along the Seaway by ship, dredging up old memories for me of the horrible twenty-two day trip from San Diego to Japan. We then flew back to Cherry Point where I vacillated between the band and administrative duties.

With the Marine Corps Band in Buffalo, New York.

With the Marine Corps Band in Cleveland, Ohio.

New orders were cut for me to report to another place, which would prove to be significant in my life. There was a small air station located at Edenton, North Carolina, which was about to be deactivated and would require personnel to phase out Marine Corps activities, including an almost obsolete Corsair squadron. This was my first real taste of air wing operations and seemed to be a departure from my experiences in "grunt" dynamics of infantry and logistics units. Things were more "laid back." Rank distinctions did not seem to be the big issues. Aviators were aware that their welfare and safety depended, very basically, on those who kept the "birds" in the air, and they related to them accordingly.

Edenton is located a very short drive from Elizabeth City, North Carolina, both in northeast North Carolina near the Virginia border. Edenton, not being a military town, as such, was not well prepared to provide housing to the small contingent of Marines and sailors stationed there. The result was a high degree of difficulty in finding adequate housing for my family, and we lived in a total of four different locations in the year or so that we spent there. The last place we occupied was a double-tenant home on a busy street in Elizabeth City, where Elizabeth City State College (now "University") was located, another historically Black college in the inevitable college town. Gravity tugged at me once again to become connected with a college community. And once again I was prepared to leave the Marine Corps and take any position available on the college campus (reminiscent of my fantasies about Compton College while in Korea), no matter how menial, in order to take courses here and there. I could become an assistant to the bandmaster at Elizabeth City State, for I knew band dynamics as well as, or better than, anything I observed on campus. The possibilities were infinite, but not the practicalities. It would be difficult to extricate myself from my commitment to the Marine Corps, and more importantly, to the financial stability of my family. Such a move would have been dubious, at best. So, the fantasy faded, and I was back to closing out Edenton, having personnel's household goods shipped to new duty stations, arranging to have equipment and supplies transported to various depots. Hollins and I were among the last to vacate the premises and turn out the lights.

A part of what seemed like our reward was our opportunity to request our next duty assignment. By now, I had become increasingly interested in the Air Wing arm of the Marine Corps and thought of this as the opportunity to change my military occupational specialty. I had grandiose ideas about becoming a navigator, and so I applied for evaluation to determine where I would fit with air service. So, off to Naval Air Station Memphis for testing. My family and I would have to find temporary housing in Millington, Tennessee, for chances were that we'd be moving on after evaluation. As it turned out, I wound up in Avionics. I would be assigned to Naval Air Station, Jacksonville, Florida for several months of schooling in avionics and electronics. Based on my performance in high school, this was to be a chore for me. Aside from plane geometry, I had done miserably in all math classes in high school. And now I had to master trigonometry. This assignment was some distance from the goal I had set for navigator school, but it was also an even greater distance from the cargo handler role that had been assigned to practically all African-American Marines just a few years earlier. So, I dove in.

After some grueling weeks of instruction, I, surprisingly, finished the course with flying colors. One's final standing in the class would define the influence of one's request for permanent duty assignment. When I left California, I missed all that the culture was about and promised myself that if I ever returned to the state, I would attempt to never leave it again. I requested assignment to the Marine Corps Air Station at El Toro, California, and to my delight, was accommodated. Oh, happy day! I could hardly believe my good fortune. At that time California culture, including its foods, was not pervasive across the country. There were no national fast-food chains, such as those today, producing the tacos and burritos that I had missed as soon as I reached the east coast. Of course, it was not the food per se, but the atmosphere of California that I missed. It was a time when distinctions between the nature of race relations in the South and California appeared to be profound. Only time would teach us that the distinctions were not as clear as first imagined. The situation was analogous to the much earlier migration of Blacks from the South to New York, Chicago, Detroit, Philadelphia, Boston, and Cleveland. All turned out to be partially fulfilled dreams. For Blacks, California, more and more, is following the trends set by the northeastern migration: ethnic and racial cleavages, diminishing employment opportunities, and disparity in the political arena. It is no wonder that there is massive exodus of Blacks leaving California to return to the Southeast. For me, the bad memories that I still have of my childhood in Birmingham make such a transition totally out of the question. Perhaps, those experiences psychologically damaged me without my knowing.

19

RETURN TO CALIFORNIA

We began our automobile trip from Jacksonville to California in February 1961. It was questionable as to whether or not our old Dodge station wagon would make the almost three thousand mile trip, so I traded it in for a slightly newer Plymouth coupe, which was about all I could afford. Picture it. An older two-door automobile loaded with four lively boys and two adults, finding its way across inhospitable territory in inclement weather. It was okay, because we were returning to California and this was to be treated as an adventure. Understatement, if there ever was one.

But first, we would stop to spend some time with family in Birmingham, Juliet's old "briar patch," or "stomping grounds." By now, I had developed a history of excruciatingly painful tonsillitis so acute that on occasion I would lose consciousness. The episodes began in Japan and occurred annually like clockwork, all because I'd never had my tonsils removed. I had the misfortune of being stricken while on our visit to Birmingham, where sometimes we stayed at my mother's home and sometimes at Juliet's mother's place in the projects (See cp-12, #2). I got as sick as I had ever been with tonsillitis, running an extremely high temperature, hardly lucid, and confined to bed on hot, sweaty, extremely humid nights at Juliet's mother's home. The severity of these attacks had landed me in the hospital in Japan.

As I was writhing in misery, Juliet saw fit to go out in the mid-afternoon, dressed to the T's. I can't recall what reason she gave for leaving, but under the circumstances, being in the freedom of her playground, it would not have mattered anyway. I was in no condition to debate or, really, to care. But I started to care at about 2 am when I awakened in a cold sweat and found that she had not returned. I dragged myself out of bed and went outside and found that she had not taken our car. The night was still, except that at that moment a car carrying two people approached very slowly and was about to stop. I recognized one of the people to be Juliet and, in my delirium, confronted the car, which then sped off with both occupants. Apparently, the driver dumped her about a block away, for soon she came walking down the street.

What should I do with the anger that is building within me by the second? I am aware of what many would have done, but sometimes rationality has its problems and we wind up wondering what would have happened if we'd gone to where our emotions had taken us. It's another crapshoot, because it seems that, for other people, most irrationality goes unpunished and we wish we'd felt the freedom to act in accordance with our feelings, and less rationality. It would take many years for me to realize that my reaction had been the correct one for that time, but there have been times when I have regretted not taking more extreme action. Such would not only have been salve for the ego, but one's sense of justice requires that wrongdoers should be penalized appropriately.

But I knew instantly that this was the beginning of the long road to the end. As with most people in untenable relationships, male or female, I had no feel for a way to extricate myself. No exit plan. Or really, no real determination to exit. All through the trauma, practicality dominated my thinking, which I saw, in this instance, to be much too constraining. I had my four sons to be concerned about. I was working on a career that demanded stability. I was up to my neck in financial obligations, which is the shameful case with most military families. The bad news was that by sticking it out, there would be about seven more years of ever-worsening misery, probably for both of us, though for different reasons. The only *blue skies* that resulted were the birth of a fifth child, our first daughter, Terri.

A recurring question that is asked more today than in the 50's and 60's is "Why do women remain in abusive relationships?" The same question could also be asked about men. At least some of the same reasons given by and for women could apply to men. A frequently cited reason given by women is related to the potential for violent retaliation. Another, in the past, had to do simply with economics. Earlier on in this society many women really did marry for a living. Women such as Mama did. There were not an awful lot of options available to them. Abuse came along with their subservient status. Another reason, which is probably the most depressing of all, is the feeling that it is women's duty as wives and homemakers to take abuse. These are not likely to be reasons given by men for being unable, or unwilling, to "split the sheets." Men's reasons are most likely to revolve around what court mandated losses might accrue to them, attachment to their children, or, as in my case, simply not knowing where to begin dissolving the relationship. Given enough grief, the answer is likely to come into focus very suddenly and without forethought. Such was the case with me.

There are many crucial points in all of our lives at which the course of our destiny is determined. We play the game of "make believe" and imagining a series of "what ifs." What if I had been wise enough or reckless enough to proceed to California alone? Do I load the children into the car and leave, which would mean an ugly fight for their custody? Or do I leave them behind with someone I had already determined to be irresponsible? Was it all a matter of perspective? Was she as miserable in the relationship as I? I had no answers and simply did what was expected of me by a society that was unaware and unconcerned about the details. I am often asked why I would remain in a miserable marriage for seventeen very long years. Our society, at that time, insisted that, regardless to the circumstances, you stick with it. Surely, given time, it will get better. Seldom is that likely to happen. Intelligence informs us when we should cut our losses.

I was a little surprised that her family members who lived in the household didn't seem to admonish her for her behavior on that fateful night in her mother's house in Loveman Village. The only reproach came from her grandmother, who was a kindly, decent woman. She was livid and unforgiving with Juliet. I liked her a lot.

So with some apprehension, I collected the family and prepared for the cross-country trek to Southern California. This entailed being cognizant of the travel network known and shared by the circle of African-American Marines. There were certain routes that Blacks avoided, routes that provided no lodging or eating facilities for them, even for Blacks who had put it all on the line in warfare for this country. There were areas that were dangerous to be seen in after dark. Black families traveling by auto often had to sleep in their cars and bring along their own food or find take-out—through the back door. It was an awful and ridiculous time in this country, and one should not be deluded into believing that we are out of the woods today. The hate and prejudice has simply taken on a different look.

The slightly newer Plymouth coupe that we started out in decided that California was too far and dropped the engine in a little town in Texas called Breckenridge. A tow truck took the car to an accommodating auto repair shop whose owner connected us with a "nice colored woman who takes in roomers." I can't recall the times we have been hooked up with such sweet old women, who were alone, gracious, and quite willing to put us up temporarily. It happened in Georgia, in North Carolina, now here in Texas and this was not to be the last. We were with this lady for four days while the car was repaired, which required parts not readily available in a small town like Breckenridge. But finally we were on our way.

Because of the car problems, the trip from Alabama to California took a little better than a week. There had been tension and quiet from the time we left Birmingham. (I wondered what the children were thinking.) That pattern persisted until we reached our destination. From my point of view, the incident in Birmingham was only the tip of the iceberg. It was the manifestation of all that had transpired for years, but the first time I got a good look at it up close.

By now, the *blue skies* for me were more about getting back to California than a safe, harmonious family about to embark on a great new beginning, for I was becoming more and more fatalistic about our marriage.

It was March, 1961, and as I drove up the long stretch of Trabuco Road to the main gate at Marine Corps Air Station, El Toro, I was blown away by the majestic eucalyptus windbreak lining the street and serving to protect the now defunct orange orchards. The real magic, though, was the intoxicating aroma of orange blossoms that permeated Orange County before the massive invasion of housing tracts. It was a different time and place. Demographics were such that one could not have possibly imagined the transition that eventually took place. The composition of the population was almost entirely lily-white. As close as we were to the Mexican border, there were only a handful of Latinos (as opposed to their 76% share of Santa Ana's population today). Asians were pretty much unheard of (as opposed to almost 9% in Santa Ana and 13.6% in Orange County today). Blacks in Orange County have hovered around 2% since the 60's, but that percentage is shrinking to 1.7% currently.

With the dominance of white, ultra-conservative, John Birch Society types in Orange County, it follows that prejudice and discrimination would abound. And it did. I encountered it right off the bat as I contacted realtors to attempt to purchase a home with my meager resources and G.I. Benefits. Being somewhat practical, I made it known that I wanted something as near to the base as possible. Being the slow learner, it took me some time to notice that none of them would stop at nearby locations, and as though their cars were on autopilot, they headed straight to southwest Santa Ana, where Black folks lived. This was an area bounded by McFadden, Fairview, First Street, and Bristol Street. Before the demographic transition, this area was a pristine community, where pride of ownership took hold, and people kept their homes painted, their lawns manicured, and their children well mannered and busy in worthwhile activities. I coached Pop Warner Football and Little League Baseball in our local Jerome Park. There were local Black small businesses that were well supported by the community. Church activities were big. There was the all-important series of Black barber shops where legitimate information and gossip alike were disseminated. (I wonder where women went for their hair care. In each other's homes?) After all was said and done, this is where we wound up. The *blue skies* in this instance were that there was an intact Black community that could take care of business when critical issues arose. Of course, the bad news was that in Orange County American citizens of color could not choose where they lived, even if they could afford to do so. My solution, after opening my eyes, was to do it myself. I canvassed the areas that made sense economically and approached homes that had "for sale" signs on them. I would ring doorbells, watch draperies or blinds move, but get no response at the door. Or, on one occasion, someone did, indeed, come to the door, but explained that the person responsible for selling the place was in Europe and would return in six months. So, why the sign?

After staying with a sweet old lady on First Street for a while, we decided to rent a home on Daisy Street, which looked decent from the outside, but had numerous internal problems. Being a "fixit" kind of person, I thought we could deal with it until something better came along. At this point, I was still commuting to and from the air station, working extended hours because of exercises in the squadron, and really had very little time to do any "fixin'." After a spell, conditions became unbearable, and it was necessary to look around again. We looked at a home on Nottingham, which was for rent with the option to buy. Many earlier homeowners had gotten into the homeownership loop using this route. You rent the home for several months, and if it turns out to suit your needs, the rental monies that you have paid now would be called a down payment, and you are on your way. It is too bad that such an option is not available to young people today.

While the Daisy Street area had not been a warm, close-knit community, Nottingham was just that. There were several boys on the street that matched my sons' ages, so some long-term connections were made among them. Sports activities were becoming more and more important to them, and here were boys with the same interests. But the home, itself, did not quite do it for us, so we started to look for something to buy outright, all in the same neighborhood. While the community was well maintained by the residents, who were primarily Black, the same could not always be said about city services. Some of the same potholes that existed there then (1962) are still there better than forty-five years later. We understood that such neglect would never happen north of Seventeenth Street, where the more affluent resided.

We found an affordable little place with bat-and-board siding on Hesperian Street. The houses were obviously inexpensively built, but, again, were well kept with great neighbors. We were excited about the place and felt that it was worth every penny of the $16,000 purchase price. It had a couple of orange trees and a lemon tree, which put us in our version of heaven.

It was here that Juliet's sister and her family came to stay with us briefly as they relocated from Fort Worth, Texas. It was good having them, for the sister was like a breath of fresh air, even-tempered, industrious, and with good orientation towards family. The brother-in-law turned out to be another physical and psychological abuser. My sister-in-law brought the same pleasant atmosphere to our home that she had brought when she and her daughter came to be with us for a short while in Albany, Georgia.

This sister-in-law and my only brother-in-law, Juliet's brother, Bubba (cp-14, #1) were the in-laws most familiar with the dynamics of life in our home. Bubba lived with us in San Francisco after getting out of the Air Force, as he attended San Francisco City College and worked for the Post Office. I should have gotten the message that when others were in our home, things were far more bearable. But that does not mean that things were totally peaceful, for they also got to witness violent altercations, for which I was completely embarrassed, being in the presence of rational people.

It was also in this home on Hesperian that Juliet decided she needed to see a therapist. While she was right in her assessment, and I do not recall her reasons for the assessment, the outcome presented another major catastrophe in our lives. She had just enough extraordinary intelligence to get herself into trouble. She attempted to play head games with an unscrupulous psychiatrist in Santa Ana. Guess who won? At about that time, there was a rash of such abuses in Orange County by psychiatrists, and she got caught in the web of one north of Seventeenth Street. She didn't stand a chance. One can only imagine what went on in their little footsie sessions. Because he was using vulgar language in his sessions, she assumed that he was attracted to her and that he wanted to marry her. That being the case, why shouldn't she round up the children and head for Los Angeles with her mother as she figured how to make it work? (All of this came out later in my presence with a legitimate therapist.)

I came home from work one day and everyone was gone. I waited around nervously for some time and finally called her mother's home in Los Angeles and learned that they were all there. I received very little explanation, except that a divorce was in order. I was concerned about my children who were pulled out of school and spirited away from their comfort zone to some place they didn't want to be. I only knew that the talk of divorce had come much too late and would have been welcomed at several other stages, for instance, upon my return from Korea. Maybe I should not have been shocked by anything at this point, but I was and had to bear down and work through it. No plan that I would devise could be pain-free and smooth. I was trying to go to school and was working full time.

The children solved that part of the problem for me. It started with Ronnie, the eldest, saving his lunch money for several days until he had enough for bus fare to Santa Ana, at which point he showed up at the front door. After that, Johnny followed Ronnie's lead and returned home. The boys and I were at home alone now. While carrying a full load at school and working full time, I managed to keep things afloat. I washed the clothes, fed the children, kept the house picked up, got the children off to school, and wondered why things were not always done that way. Juliet and I continued to talk and, for whatever reason, she agreed that she should come back, and I was to come to get her.

At this point, all the reasons to be angry that had built up over the years were put aside in favor of family survival, which, first of all, meant looking into Juliet's psychological issues. On the way from Los Angeles to Santa Ana, she suddenly said that she'd lost it and needed immediate help. I stopped at Norwalk State Hospital where she was seen, diagnosed, and sent her on her way to be evaluated at what was then the County of Orange Hospital (now UCI). They diagnosed schizophrenia and kept her for seventy-two hours, after which she would have to go before a judge who would make a decision regarding disposition of her case. I pleaded that she be released to my custody, to which the judge agreed, provided that I seek competent, reputable therapy for her. I sought out a psychiatrist in La Habra who was reputed to be trustworthy and professional. Now came the revelations. It seemed that I had been modest in my estimation of the harm that she had done to herself and to this relationship. By now, I was personally saturated and immune to future hurt at her hands. I now moved into a protective mode on her behalf. I suppose after so much emotional involvement, you don't turn it off, as with a spigot. I suppose no one should ever do anything that he or she would not want to surface in therapy. The revelations were beyond belief.

Although too much information was coming to light, which gave the new psychiatrist a lot to work with, the demons did not seem to go away. He then resorted to something that I had always thought to be barbaric and out of vogue. She went through electroshock therapy, designed to reduce depression. One shortfall of the therapy is that the problem often recurs after a time, putting the patient back to square one. The therapy was a last-ditch effort, since all else had been unsuccessful. The treatment was unsuccessful as well. In a few months, we were back where we started.

In the meantime, we were necessarily coping with day-to-day activities, with me always waiting for the other shoe to drop. I was continuing to go to school, which got to be harder and harder as conflicts with my military duties became more and more frequent. The deployment to temporary duty in Yuma became more problematic on several fronts. The immediate concern was the fear that, in Juliet's state of mind, things at home would be in jeopardy. The children were well mannered and relatively obedient. My feeling was that there was a good chance that that would not be enough. Also, there was the problem of my missing too much school. These two issues, along with the nagging feeling that my life was on a treadmill, caused me to have serious thoughts about making a rather drastic life change. In addition, our squadron was scheduled for deployment overseas in a few months, and I had no doubt that nothing short of a disaster would result for my family. All of this prompted me to write a letter to Headquarters, Marine Corps, explaining that I had performed dutifully for better than eleven years, in spite of the difficulties for my family, but things were at the point where my presence in the home had become crucial for their welfare. I, therefore, respectfully requested to be released from my commitment to further service. I was elated when word came back that my request had been granted. However, the chaos that I had feared by remaining in the Marines could not be avoided. Things would only get worse with my marriage.

The response came quickly and, actually, as a shock. Therefore, I had made no preparations for a future as a civilian. The process of becoming a civilian after twelve years in the Marine Corps is not an easy or a sudden one. It took me, easily, a year and a half to become fully in charge of myself, to make my own decisions, and to not be constrained by geographical boundaries. It felt as though I had one foot in civilian life, with the other in combat boots.

The lone certainty in my plans was school. I could not wait, although I knew that, as a thirty-one year-old freshman, it would be a long haul and that I would be much older than most of the college-going population. But I didn't care. This was my shot, and I intended to make the most of it. I knew that Mama would be proud and that her legacy would live on. The path that I had taken out of high school had somehow landed me here. My only continuing regret was that Bay-Suh had been robbed of the opportunity to pursue higher education, for I always felt that she possessed superior potential. She attempted to pursue college work at Miles College in Birmingham, only to have the support rug pulled from under her by broken promises from our father.

I have always been obsessed with economic stability, no matter the level. As I contemplated the future during adolescence, the ideal career included such jobs as mail carrier or almost any type of civil service work. None of the jobs were get-rich-quick schemes, especially as I view them in retrospect. But as I looked around in my community, these were the employees who appeared most secure. Even many service jobs, such as Pullman porters, were highly regarded by a lot of community people, primarily because the jobs were clean and steady. Having made no plans for my separation from the Marine Corps, I had done nothing in the way of job seeking. I had given no thought to my qualifications for work in civilian life (or lack of same). I had musical skills, but by now I was bright enough to know that if I was not among the very best in the field, I should be smart enough not to subject myself to such a miserable existence. Witness the shelf life of many of the best in the business.

I had wonderful training in electronics and avionics, as indicated by my assignment as quality assurance sign-off individual for my jet squadron, a role that gained me a lot of friends among the young pilots. These were probably the most marketable skills that I brought to the table, but using those skills was not something that I really wanted to do. So, I went for something safe that would give me ample opportunity to attend school without interruption. I took two clerical exams, one for the postal service and the other for the local gas company. I passed them both and now had to make a choice between them. Having spent so much time in the civil service-like environment, I decided to go the other way, knowing that either choice would embed me in a bureaucracy. But in today's society, that would be all but inevitable. The Gas Company seemed to test for passivity, wanting people who would go along to get along. I always wondered how I managed to get in, for I had always seen myself as an extrovert (though now I know better). Maybe their test told me something about myself that I did not know, for I have since learned that I am actually an introvert. In spite of my sometimes overactive mouth, I am not comfortable with large crowds and excessive verbiage. I think that I made some of the higher-ups a little uncomfortable with my ready greetings and my propensity for small talk. I attribute those tendencies to nervous energy or hyperactivity.

My tenure at the Gas Company was seven years. I started out as a mail clerk, which put me all over the place, talking to too many people, becoming familiar with the "lay of the land." The company was just about as conservative as it gets. So it is no wonder that my style and persona rubbed a few people the wrong way. But I was a conscientious and dependable worker, which took care of any other problems I might have presented. Most of the staff were really encouraging about my school efforts and never let up on the nudging. This came at a time when encouragement was vital for me, for the school and workloads were exceptionally demanding.

After the stint as mail clerk, I noticed that the ideal job available to me at that stage was the meter reader position. When a position became available, I applied and was given the assignment, which worked well with my school schedule. A meter reader, typically, is given eight hours worth of work to complete each day. After completing the assigned route, even if less than eight hours, the reader's work day is finished. I was short and fast. I could generally complete an eight-hour route in four hours and felt confident in scheduling classes beginning at one in the afternoon. There were a number of benefits that accrued to meter readers. One of the more important ones related to health issues. Walking (running, actually) was excellent exercise, and it was a rare sight to see an overweight reader. Another advantage was the requirement to cover the entire county over a period of time. Gas meters tend to stay put for interminable lengths of time. Consequently, the locations of those that I was familiar with decades ago are virtually the same today. I got to know the geography of all the segments of the county, the demographics of all the cities and communities, and the problems inherent in any area lacking in diversity. I will always remember a little boy on a tricycle in Yorba Linda following me along my route as I moved from house to house. He'd always be waiting for me as I emerged from between the houses. When I reached the corner and was about to cross the street, I asked him if his mother knew where he was and shouldn't he go back home now. He looked up at me and, with a smile that only a child can muster, said, "Mister, you're a dirty nigger." I knelt down on one knee and asked him where he'd heard that. He said, "My daddy says that, and sometimes my mommy says it too."

In the sixties, there were still areas in Orange County where especially young people had had little exposure to people unlike themselves. I witnessed and was subjected to a good example of the absurd consequence of provincialism. Enrichment meant "more of the same." Nowhere have I seen "fear of the unknown" more prevalent, and I had lived in what I considered to be the most segregated conditions in the country in Birmingham. There was too much of a tendency to expect that conditions would be improved outside of that environment, but this is a mistake historically made by Blacks as they migrated north and west to escape the harshness of blatant prejudice and discrimination in the South. Things turned out to be only slightly better, as the difference was in form, not substance.

Later on, I became a dispatcher at the Gas Company, where my latter day very best friend, George Woods, and I sorted and scheduled work orders and routed the servicemen for the next day. We worked from three-thirty pm to midnight, taking phone calls from disgruntled, non-pay customers who had had their service discontinued during the day. This was an experience in itself. Irate people who threatened to call in their "corps of lawyers" would keep the phones ringing off the hook once they got home and discovered that they'd been shut down. Maybe George had been dealing with them too long, for he had little tolerance for what he called "dead-beats." He would often let his feelings be known to the customers and invariably would have to write explanations to our supervisors Monday mornings after hectic weekends. Upon being harassed by an abusive customer, he once told him, "Oh, go fry your ass" and slammed down the receiver. George's chaser after such an encounter was a swig of Maalox, which he kept handy for the occasion. It was not unusual to see him heading for the board room with yellow legal pad tucked under his arm to compose his defense to the charges that were always sure to come in first thing the next morning.

But our workstation was not all bad, nor was it all serious. I certainly had not grown out of my deviant tendencies, and George was even more deviant, along with being more clever. So, the stage was set to break the killer monotony after the work was done. Our supervisor was of German extraction and was bent on order and precision. That presented a problem for him, for we were bent on breaking down order and precision. He had replaced the company wall clock with his own. He often touted the superiority of German engineering. Maybe he was right. But we were determined to prove him wrong. So, every night we would take his clock off the wall and turn it back a minute or so. The morning people would report to us how he would look at it in wonderment, remove it from the wall, take it to his desk and proceed to dismantle it with his screwdriver, and when satisfied replace it on the wall, only to have it go through the same process again the following night.

To mix it up a bit, we would lower his chair one turn each night, until finally his chin would be near his desktop. We also heard that he expounded on the virtue of German auto engineering, specifically the Volkswagen, "The people's car." He mentioned not only that it was superior to American cars, but also that "You never see Negroes driving them." At that moment, I drove my newly acquired Bug up to the plate glass window to show my handful of co-workers. The supervisor, who just happened to be standing at the window, clicked his heels, turned and headed for his desk in disgust.

With encouragement from my co-workers and a work schedule that was forgiving, I managed to get the bachelor's degree in Anthropology completed in 1969. I earned the Master's degree one year later in 1970. Not bad for a D average high school goof-off. It was fortunate that the encouragement came from some other source, for it certainly was not coming from home. In fact, I was getting continuous discouragement from my wife. "What are you doing that for?" "What are you trying to prove?" The problem was that she had taken some credits while I was in Korea, and it became a problem when I passed the number of units she had earned while playing cheer leader. It was totally impossible to convince her that this was about *us*, about the well-being of the family and not mostly about me. The concept totally escaped her. There was a ton of projection going on with her for she was viewing what she would do, and had done, under the same circumstances. Remember Miles College?

20

THE MELTDOWN

The situation with the family was totally disintegrating. My wife's contempt and lack of support for my efforts at work and at school seemed to get worse day by day. I was the sole wage earner for the most part. There was a period when she worked at a job in the fiscal area for the County of Orange. But her attitude was that she could go to work if she chose, or not if she chose not to. Her tenure there didn't last very long. But the biggest problem was not that she did not contribute to the family's budget, but that she set out consciously to prevent me from doing so. She made it clear that she would "ruin me." I made the mistake of earning the income, but leaving the responsibility for actually paying the bills to her. They didn't get paid. I would receive calls from creditors at my job asking when they could expect payments. I would then find loose cash lying around in drawers. At the same time, she was making major clothing purchases from some of the nicer clothing stores for no purpose other than hanging them in closets with the tags intact.

The relationship was in its final stages. I found myself on about three occasions sitting with elbows on the bar having beers in cheap beer joints in Santa Ana. This was not characteristic of me, and I began to feel disjointed and out of sorts. Arguments at home began to become more frequent and more caustic. They were more like the violent situations that upset me so as a child. Simply put, I was miserable. And I have to believe that she had to be, as well. There had to be something missing in her life that she really wanted, a lifestyle born of negative indulgence. Things were simply too sedate for her, given her past.

After one such exchange, I thought I'd just walk out the door, hoping to defuse the matter, at least temporarily. But before I got to the door, an electric iron caught me in the right shoulder, and although it was not terribly painful, it gave me only a short time to decide how I should react. Of course, the first inclination was to react in kind and return the favor. But somehow I had the presence of mind to know that such a reaction would only make bad matters worse, for me. So, I got into my car and drove away. Little did I know and appreciate that it would be for good. I had no idea where I was going and wound up checking into a cheap, transient motel on Fourth Street in Santa Ana where people came and went every hour on the hour it seemed. I hibernated there for a full week, no shaves, virtually no meals, and no reporting to work. I pondered my next move, still having no clear sense of how one extricates oneself, given responsibilities for children and bills and such. By the time that I emerged at the end of the week, I had reached one certainty: I would never, under any circumstances, return to

Juliet, though she was cruelly assuring the children that I would tire of my situation outside and come to my senses. She was right. I had finally come to my senses, but the outcome was not what she expected. And I wished that she had not made that promise to children who were already in an awkward and confused position. The logistics of calling it quits were too muddled to work out in my present state. So, some power far bigger than I took over, and for the first time in my life, I can't remember consciously making the ultimate decision. That power took the control completely out of my hands. The complications would just have to work themselves out. It was the first time in my adult life that I felt totally bereft of direction.

I got myself a little apartment in Garden Grove that was affordable and very clean. It was the first bit of peace that I had enjoyed in years. I made every effort to see the children, or have them over as often as allowed. By now there were five. Terri was born after I left, and I have always believed that Juliet was using that pregnancy as cement for a failing marriage. The *blue skies* were that it produced Terri, who carried on the drive and determination of Mama. After several attempts at gaining custody of the children, I was finally successful with Terri, and she eventually lived with us where she graduated from Saddleback College. She later graduated from Cal State Northridge, which will be discussed later.

In the midst of this volatile period, I met my current wife, Suzanne. One of the new things I learned about myself was that, in spite of my appreciation for my newfound peace, I could not at that time stand to be alone. When a bunch of us guys from the Gas Company got off from work at midnight, we would head for a little beer, shuffleboard, popcorn, and song at a little place in Orange called The Salty Dawg. When the place closed at two a.m., I was sad to see my friends go off to their homes as I headed for an empty apartment.

The experience has served me well in teaching Marriage and Family classes. My situation, trying to make progress with Juliet, was like having an anchor tied to your drive so that you continually question yourself and whether you are doing the right thing. Just try to function to your capacity under those conditions. I have witnessed innumerable, especially older and female, students who are trying to make it happen under such constraints. Many withdraw out of frustration.

O.K. At this point I had this bachelor's degree in hand. What should I do with it? Did the Gas Company have me in mind for management? I didn't think so. In fact, I didn't feel comfortable with that prospect, considering the culture. So, I took a job with the state of California Employment Development Department, with an eye to becoming an Employment Services Officer. Unfortunately, it turned out to be similar to the environment that I had become familiar with in the Marine Corps with Civil Service workers. There were scores of people working there who seemed to be marking time. Many had already retired from the military and were poised to double-dip, or even triple-dip, by getting one more retirement. In other words, the place was wallowing in lethargy. Some co-workers asked me why I didn't slow down. Almost immediately I knew that this was not going to work for me. If I hung around too long, I'd become like what I was seeing.

But not all of the staff were laggards. In fact, the manager was a forward-looking, energetic sort who tried to assemble a like-minded crew. He half succeeded. The state had just launched this wonderful concept of the "Job Agent," which was a position designed to make a marriage between the chronically unemployed and prospective employers. This provided another layer of insight for me. Never again would I simply assume that anyone who wants to work could get a job. The longer a person is out of the job market, the tougher it is to break in again. Employers would consider not only the idle stretches, but also such things as currency of one's dress or whether or not one has personal transportation. (Never mind that public transportation might be more dependable than a bundle of nuts and bolts that sometime are not on the same page.) Employers' attitudes were "Why should I hire someone that no one else has been willing to hire? After all, I am not in the rehabilitation business. It's all about profit margin." Occasionally, though, it would happen and there would emerge an employer capable of mixing compassion with good business sense.

I am the sole survivor of the three blacks on the staff. I applied for the Job Agent position, was tested, and was hired to an entry-level position on a track to become an Employment Services Officer. Tommy Crockett, the other Black male, was installed as a Job Agent. This was where the action was and where I wanted to be. But Tommy was an apparent community activist who had street-wise deportment and appearance, required qualities for a job involving getting down with the disenfranchised, as well as getting through the doors of business people. I knew that I possessed these same qualities, but they were not as apparent. My job turned out to be to deal with the clients who came through the door for services, and while all of it was meaningful, it was not as exciting and challenging as my needs required.

The other African-American there was an absolutely marvelous woman whose face always offered an infectious smile and who greeted all people as though they were the most special people on earth. Her name was Lillian Teague. From my perspective, hers was a tragic existence. Her perspective was probably more positive. She was the first person I knew who had debilitating Sickle Cell anemia, which took her out of circulation for days on end as she experienced excruciating pain and was unable to work. Her situation so affected me that I later founded an organization called The Sickle Cell Disease Research Foundation, which was designed to provide testing and counseling certainly for the 2% African-American population in Orange County, but also for anyone else who wanted the services. Lillian's horrifying experiences, though painful and debilitating, inspired the idea of the screening foundation, which heightened the community's awareness of its problem. This likely would not have happened without Lillian's suffering. *There are always blue skies.* By now, almost everyone who might be affected by this crippling disease is aware of the importance of testing and counseling prior to making marital choices and to producing children. I was guilty of assuming my own invincibility up to the age of seventy when I first learned that I am a carrier of the sickle-cell trait, which means that I am capable of passing it on, though I, myself, am not affected. The inevitable occurred when one of my grandsons came along and has continuous episodes of painful crises and consistent hospitalizations. It was amazing to me that of the dozens of dozens of times that I had been in the care of medical providers, it took seventy years for caregivers to notice that sickle cell was a factor with me. It came to light only when my physician, after reviewing routine test results said, "By the way, John, do you know that you carry the sickle-cell trait?" It is scary to imagine that literally thousands could be in the dark about sickle cell, thereby, putting future generations in jeopardy.

Tommy Crockett, my co-worker Job Agent and friend, was extraordinary. He knew the streets well and could relate comfortably with whomever. I admired him immensely, but really wanted to do what he was doing and knew that my experiences had prepared me well for the role. Tommy was another tragedy that occurred in the one year that I spent at the Human Resources Department. He was very dependable and methodical. So it was very unusual that he did not show up for work one Monday. There were all kinds of positive speculations explaining his absence. "He has a girlfriend who lives in San Diego, and he probably couldn't get back after the weekend." "He was probably in the field doing job development, or working with a client." But, really, these did not explain why he had not checked in. So when he did not show up again on Tuesday, I became concerned and went to his apartment, which was about a mile from the office. I knocked on his door several times without getting a response. Further concerned, I got in touch with the apartment manager to have him open Tommy's door. As soon as the door was cracked, we knew the obvious. The aroma of death almost knocked us backwards. We found Tommy lying face down in his bed, smothered in his pillow. Tommy had epilepsy and had taken it upon himself to discontinue his medication some time ago. Apparently, he had a grand mal seizure and was unable to turn over. There is a basic lesson here about leaving medical decisions to those who are supposed to know and understand medicine. Tommy had expressed that he was tired of being a prisoner to his regimen. I doubt that he would have preferred death to that detested regimen. The feeling of invincibility isn't something unique to the young.

21

THE ROAD
TO ACADEME

In the meantime, a wonderful Dean of Instruction at Santa Ana College, Dr. Vernon Armstrong, whom I had known when I attended there as a thirty-one-year-old freshman, asked me to teach a course there in Black History. While I didn't know much about history, pedagogically, I knew a lot about being Black. And consequently that somehow translates to history. With a lot of research and reading, I got up to speed quickly. I not only did a pretty good job with the course, but also actually enjoyed teaching and looked forward to meeting the class once a week.

This was the era of student activism, and all around the country, students were demonstrating and making demands regarding relevance of curriculum. While much of the rhetoric was pure hogwash, just as much of it made good sense. There was the clamor for Ethnic Studies, which made more than good sense because in this multi-ethnic society very few of the contributions of ethnic minorities had been disseminated to the population at large. Most Blacks, especially those reared in the South pre-nineteen fifty, can remember a book written by Carter G. Woodson entitled *Negro History*. Even that book was somewhat limited in scope, though Dr. Woodson was responsible for a number of books revealing what had been omitted in much of American history. He was also noted for founding Black History Month.

The rhetoric that was nonsense can be forgiven, for it was made mostly out of ignorance and frustration. That part of the rhetoric demanded that only those courses that interested the students be offered and that they contain only what students desired. Little or no thought had been given to making students well rounded, which is a quality conspicuous for its absence in society today. We have, unfortunately, become a nation of specialists, an issue subjected to considerable debate. For better than a hundred years, since the industrial revolution impacted us, we have become increasingly specialized, to the extent that we can do only what our specialty has trained us to do. Get us out of our element and we are lost. The good news for old-timers is that our comprehensive backgrounds have increased in relative value. Look around and notice who the consultants are. They are more likely to possess the lost art of interpersonal communication skills.

The racial minority students at Santa Ana College wanted Black Studies and Chicano Studies. The college had been in existence since 1915, and in fifty-five years had never had an African-American faculty member and only one Hispanic. Now, because of the noises being made by Black and Latino students, it was necessary for the college to scurry about and find a Black to work with the only existing Hispanic staffer to get Ethnic Studies off the ground. Because the pressure was brought by the Black Students' Union, the process for potential faculty members was to meet with the students and the Dean of instruction to be interviewed. My interview was interesting and I felt that it went well. I left the room afterwards, leaving the BSU and the Dean to discuss me. I learned later that the beret and H. Rap Brown-type glasses wearing leader offered, "I don't think he's our boy." He had more of a dubious history than I, so I wound up Chairman of the Black Studies Department. The students and I had a great run for three years, developing curriculum, selecting new part-time faculty, and putting on cultural events. (See cp-13, #2).

After one year with the State of California Employment Department, I resigned to take a full-time faculty position at the college, at a cut in pay. I was convinced that it was a good move for me, for I had gotten a sense of exceptional satisfaction whenever I walked away from a session with the one class that I had taught. That job satisfaction, coupled with a relatively new marriage, seemed too good to be true, but time would prove my new job to be as good as it seemed.

I had never been involved with such wonderful, close-knit in-laws, except for Bubba. My new mother-in-law was unbelievably supportive of me. We seemed to click from day one. I miss her dearly. I could pursue my work and school without looking over my shoulder and wondering if what I was doing was inappropriate, as my former wife continually reminded me. I was way over my head in bills, for at the interlocutory hearing I was asked by the judge what my take-home pay was. When I responded, he said, "That's how much I order you to give to her." Foolishly, I asked, "But how am I to support myself so as to be able to work?" To which he said, "It's either that or there's a jail right across the street." It would be some time before I learned what I thought was the reason for the coldness.

After I had been away from the home for a couple of weeks, I felt that it was time to put the stamp of finality on the separation. I thought I'd be the gentleman and allow Juliet to be the one to file for divorce, and suggested as much. It was a way of letting her save face. Six months later when I was suing for custody, having dispatched two incompetent attorneys and serving as my own attorney (in pro per), I dug into the divorce file and learned what she had alleged in her complaint. I could not believe my eyes as I read that I was woman chaser, a poor provider, and that she was "afraid for her life," stock divorce attorneys' key phrases. The lesson here was that it does not pay to attempt to be nice, as most attorneys are likely to advise. The tendency among most men who want a divorce, according to my attorney friends, is to give too much upon splitting up, probably mostly out of guilt, or maybe out of paternalism. I did not have a guilt problem. In fact, I wondered how it would be possible to do what I was accused of, given my work load, school schedule, and commitment to my children.

The way I would support myself in the interim, until the one-year interlocutory period was up, was to work a lot of overtime, a lot of part-time extra jobs, and to eat a lot of cheap hamburgers. However, the other significant thing that I was not accustomed to was a new wife who poured her income into the mix, providing immeasurable relief for a burden of child support with no end in sight. In addition, she understood my devotion to my children and treated them as her own. By the way, I had more success serving as my own attorney than I did with trained horrible ones. I did the whole process on my own, including typing my own subpoenas and having them served. Granted, the judge gave me a bit of latitude, being the novice that I was.

In order to not impose on Sue's generosity, I often worked a job and a half while attending school. On one occasion, I worked two full-time jobs and school, the Gas Company from three-thirty to midnight, Delco Battery Factory in Buena Park from midnight to eight in the morning, and on to school—fifteen units worth. Now, I'm one who requires eight hours of sleep, and I obviously wasn't getting it. So, the factory job didn't last very long, just long enough for me to doze on the assembly line and acquire a scar on my forearm, which I still carry as a reminder of the toughest of times. So, I discarded my steel-toed shoes and union membership and scaled back to my usual sixty-hour workweek. When students whine to me about carrying a 12-unit load and working half time, I have to restrain myself from laughing in their faces. People do what they have to do.

There is no magical set of coping skills for getting through the most challenging and troubling times. I have been convinced that different strategies work for different people. But I also believe that the most enduring and successful antidote to trauma, tragedy, or seemingly insurmountable obstacles is hard work. You put your nose to the grindstone, as it were, and keep your head down and focused on the task at hand, for if you look up and assess your situation, you are more likely to perceive hopelessness and throw in the towel. One's character has much to do with one's reaction to challenges. Some feel put upon and feel that adversity is unique to them. They then spend their energies whining and making excuses for their predicament.

Others see adversity as a challenge to be dealt with, or they don't have the sense to be intimidated or discouraged. It has become very clear to me that hard work and time are the equalizers and that those who twiddle their thumbs waiting for good things to happen to them will be left in the dust. All other things being equal, hard workers will likely prevail.

My years at Santa Ana College provided lessons for me about the nature of bureaucracy that set the stage for later enlightenment in the business of education. Make no mistake about it. I was brought in to satisfy a need at that time. I was not the messiah, come to solve fifty-five years of problems. Had it not been for the ruckus made by the Black students, there is a very good chance that I never would have landed at the college. I brought no special academic background, just varied life experiences mixed with a goodly amount of formal academic training, which worked well to educate diverse adult students.

But never mind how and why I arrived there. I was there and the role seemed to fit like a glove. I was determined that this was it for me, and that I would be here in some capacity for the duration. And the capacities were

Jammin' with the students at Santa Ana College.

145

many. What started out as a part-time teaching position in history evolved into a full-time Anthropology and Sociology professorship. From that I moved to Director in Student Services, to Associate Dean of Student Services, to Dean of Student Services, to Department Chair in Social Sciences, to Division Chair, all concurrent with my teaching, and now to serving as Chair of Social Sciences and Professor of Anthropology and Sociology.

My stint as founding chair of the Black Studies Department occurred at the height of the years of student activism and was a challenge for anyone attempting to find that thin line between raw emotion and reason. My life experiences necessarily made me give some rein to raw emotion, but those same experiences told me that there was plenty of room for reason in the equation. In fact, neither approach would work without the presence of the other. The blend worked well, for most of us involved in the process were open to divergent ideas. We became involved in critical thinking before it was fashionable. We all learned that we didn't know it all. I don't believe that I have ever worked with more dedicated and mannerly students than those in the Black Student's Union. I can't help but believe, and certainly hope, that those same qualities have followed them wherever they are today. If so, these would be the *blue skies* out of a very tempestuous and confrontational period. There were, however, a couple of students among them who saw fit to give me a hard time because of my interracial marriage.

22

NEW BEGINNINGS

My relationship with my wife, Suzanne, began while we were both employed at the Gas Company. The two students who had a problem with us did so because Sue is Caucasian. While I would never make apologies for our marriage, the reason for it made a lot of sense. I was in a culture where my pool of eligibles was pretty much restricted to Whites, and, actually, I never gave any thought to the choice that we made, for it all seemed like a natural progression of things. The lack of sophistication and experience on the part of the two female students gave them little to work with, and they saw everything in the proverbial black and white. This was a non-issue with the rest of the students, although the disgruntled two attempted to make it an issue with them as well. After all, we were getting done what needed to be done, and, for them, that was all that mattered. By the way, some time afterwards, one of the two students (the leader and most upset one) who expressed the most concern with Sue and me would later experience her African-American mother marrying a Caucasian gentleman. And by all appearances, she was supportive of their union.

Considering my earlier years in Birmingham, one would expect me to be super-sensitive to racial matters, especially society's perception and treatment of the institution of segregation. Somewhere in my travels, I got lost and ceased to be personally concerned about racial differences. Oh, I was not naïve enough to be unaware of how that institution of double standards is at work almost everywhere one looks. But I had ceased to be intimidated by it. I think that what I had witnessed since childhood, as I subconsciously noticed where I stood in the context of all those around me, taught me that I shaped up pretty well by comparison. At least I had nothing to be ashamed of. Long before I became familiar with Leo Buscaglia, the great educator, I bought into his notion of what he described as the "Democratic Character, that there is nobody better or worse than we are." That is where I am today. While I feel strongly that there is no one worse than I, I feel just as confident that there is not a single person on earth, man or woman, who is better than I. Of course, we have different talents and natural abilities, and because of different opportunities in life, what we are capable of accomplishing is also likely to produce different results. Racial differences produce varying consequences, but only because of the sociological definition of race. I realize that it is dangerous to get lured into idealizing human relations in this society. It sets you up for disappointment after disappointment unless the will is abnormally strong.

After the incident with the two female students and a few whispers in public, I suppose there was just enough paranoia in me to wonder if our marriage was at issue in other decisions made that impacted our lives. At first, such thoughts did not even occur to me. But a few things, such as our difficulty in renting apartments and overheard snide remarks questioning, "Why couldn't she have found a nice white boy? There must be lots of them around," made me wonder. The comments were made loud enough to ensure that we heard them. And while the remarks stung a bit, I felt that they were more a reflection of redneck mentality than of us as a couple of strong individuals who were dedicated to each other. There is still some residue of that kind of thinking throughout the society today, though either significantly reduced or hidden below the surface. In any case, it is a non-issue with me, for I feel that if others are so preoccupied with my relationship, then there is probably something being neglected in their own. It is enough of a hassle to mind one's own business. Few of us are capable of handling polygamy effectively. Being the typical know-it-all adolescent, I did not take to heart much of the valuable advice Mama gave me, most often subtly. But one thing that I did listen to (probably because it made sense to me, but also because it seemed defiant) was the notion that I should not be too concerned about the opinions of others. Her thinking was that as you are writhing in agony, fretting about what others think, they've probably moved on and are making someone else's life miserable. Also, it is quite possible that they had no regard for you in the first place, one way or another. The damage is done by our own imaginations and perceptions, whether true or not. For all intents and purposes, they might just as well be true if we internalize them. Obviously, there is a line beyond which self-confidence can be hazardous. Cockiness is the stuff of which psychopaths are often made. Sanity and rationality are what helps to keep that line in focus. Oh, how often I have wished that I might be more irrational and behave according to emotion's dictates. But then someone surely would have been hurt and, consequently, so would I. Beginning with the infamous stop in Birmingham en route to southern California.

My former wife certainly wasn't about to let me off the hook with an interracial marriage. The children would hear of it often. The attitudes of some of them would be shaped by the vitriolic discourse they continually heard. If I was expecting the worse, I was not disappointed. I ran into the venom again in court scenes. My new, interracial marriage was good reason for me to be denied custody of my children. Never mind that they were in perhaps the worse situation possible with their mother. The courts determined that. The routine in custody cases was to evaluate the homes of both parents to determine "what is in the best interest of the children." The investigation concluded that my home, far and away, was the most ideal situation for them. This experience, along with the awful decision made at the interlocutory stage, convinced me that judges have far too much latitude in rendering decisions. What is worse, some are so arbitrary as to be outside of what the law intended. I will always remember an arrogant judge reacting to my positive evaluation with "I know that the father is better prepared to care for the children, but I'm going to 'give' them to the mother." My family, especially the children, would pay dearly for that totally inappropriate and paternalistic decision. Perhaps one of the best things that has happened with regards to California's domestic relations cases was to move from the "divorce" designation to "dissolution of marriage." The prevailing thought among many is that dissolution of marriage (or no-fault) has heightened the divorce rate. But these are people who obviously have not been stung by a system that requires a plaintiff and a defendant, which translates to someone who has been wronged and someone who committed the wrong. It does not get much uglier than one party needing to come up with nasty charges, often manufactured, only for the respondent to react in kind with even nastier countercharges. Often, when children are involved, they get caught in the middle and are asked to choose allegiances and function as couriers to transmit information back and forth while reporting on unusual occurrences "over there." What is usually looked for is positive change in lifestyle, such as new relationships or new furnishings or automobiles. And just as often, children learn early how to play one end against the other and give each parent what he or she wants in return for certain rewards.

I doubt if the outcome would have been different if an African-American judge had been sitting on the bench for our proceedings. It's a judge thing. But it bothered me even more that, once again, white males were controlling the destiny of Black families without knowing or caring about the repercussions of their decisions and working with assembly-line "justice," not fully understanding the total situation. They could not possibly have foreseen the tragedies that were to follow. Nor would they have cared. This was just another shiftless, slick African-American male who was less than industrious to the extent of being irresponsible. And here was another dominant African-American female who, though holding everything together, was saddled with an ineffectual male and, at the same time, had reason to "fear for her life." It was all a classic example of the danger of stereotypes. I wondered how many other African-American men had suffered as a result of misconceptions or outright contempt.

I sometimes fantasize, after the fact, about how the dissolution of our marriage might have gone in the era of no-fault. There might not have remained the terrible feelings of antipathy that persisted throughout the years. The children would have fared far better if the false accusations had not made for an extremely contentious environment of which they were a part. Regardless to what had transpired in the family before, how do children choose alliances? Why should they have to? Such a situation stifles communication, which is just as crucial at the breakup of a marriage as it is in the marriage itself, especially where children are involved. I must admit that as a result of the damage done to the relationship, before and after the divorce, I was not very conciliatory and had no desire to establish or maintain communication in any form with my former wife. It was a bitter divorce and I strongly suspect that the feelings were mutual. None of this served to make things easier for the children, and, true to form, some chose to take sides. If, at the time, I had had a better understanding of the principles of successful divorces, I would have made serious attempts at "sucking it up" and tried to swallow my pain and pride for the sake of the children. Under the circumstances, considering the person with which I was dealing, I doubt seriously if any attempt that I would have made towards conciliation would have mattered. And at this point, I really didn't want to ever get back with her, anyway. But I would have liked an amicable divorce, which was not to be. She was who she was. In a more ideal world, I wish I could at least have made the attempt. But by this time, I had reached my absolute limit. I had no reason to believe that the relationship could possibly be improved. And it never was.

The *blue skies* hovering over tumultuous earthbound and seemingly insurmountable problems were many. I doubt that those beautiful skies can compensate for *all* the downsides of this family's journey. However, I feel well armed to fully understand the ups and downs of family life and its cycles. I should think that someone who has known only the ideal would not be as prepared to deal with the reality of the peaks and valleys that are inevitable in marital relationships. A basic tenet in marital relationships is that conflict is inevitable, even under the best of circumstances. Strong, stable relationships make it possible to withstand problems. I know that I would not be as prepared for the marriage and family classes that I teach and for my current relationship if I had not experienced rough times first hand. And I do not wish the negatives on anyone, for not everyone who experiences them may necessarily survive. I suppose the trick is to be oblivious to the possibilities of treachery and deceit. But is ignorance really bliss? Consider the price that I paid for inaction.

During and after the interlocutory period, I not only attempted to see my children as often as possible, but also sought custody of them on three occasions. I began to become very concerned about their well-being, realizing that their best interest would not be served in their present situation. My attempts were not well received by my former wife or by many in her family. I think that should have been expected. But those who knew the dynamics of our family were in a position to know what would have been best for the children. It probably boiled down to a matter of family loyalty, on their part, above all else. There is no comparison to the thickness of blood to that of water. I have to believe, then, that the emphasis was more on loyalty than on what was truly in the best interest of dependent children. I was disappointed because in the process I lost what I had thought were rational in-law friends. But the loss was not total. I retained the valued friendship of my brother-in-law, "Bubba" Grattan. I call him "Bubba" because in southern vernacular, "Bubba" means. affectionately, "Brother." That friendship has persisted over the years and will continue to do so. He has been unflappable in his devotion to me and rational regarding family dynamics. He and his wife Gloria are gems. (See cp-14, #1).

I feel comfortable that I ran the gamut in attempting to properly prepare the children to deal with the divorce. Most of my assurances were classic. "You guys had absolutely nothing to do with our decision to split." "We both love you and will continue to do so for always." "It is really important that you be supportive of your mother. She'll need it." "I will always be accessible to you," (in spite of their mother's request that I relocate, for my continued presence was embarrassment to her). Of course, I refused to disappear and made every attempt to either collect them for visits, gain custody of them, or to have them spend extended times with me. Over the years, all of them spent time residing in my home, some for short periods of time and some for years.

For some of the children the attempts at preparation for the inevitable divorce made sense. For others, no amount of preparation on my part to make them understand my commitment to them would have effect, for the maternal influence was too powerful. This was troubling to me, for how do you combat such influences without reacting in kind? Negative reaction could only cause more confusion for the children. My eldest son, Ronnie, was probably the most adversely affected. In keeping with conventional theory, of all the children, his world would suffer the most disruption. His grounding was the most solidly and securely fixed. He was eighteen years old at the time of the divorce, and life, as he knew it, came to a screeching halt. Without me in the household, he saw himself assuming my role as protector, an assumption that would have tragic consequences.

John, Jr., my number two son, was definitely negatively impacted, for he had been more of an achiever than Ronnie and was involved in a number of extracurricular activities, including band (The Santa Ana Westwinds), Pop Warner Football, and Little League Baseball. I coached both football and baseball. John was also involved in scouting activities. While there was some disruption in these activities, John and I remained extremely close; in fact, he lived with us in Anaheim for several years and graduated from Katella High School in 1970. Parents, generally, in the process of conducting day-to-day family activities, do not catch little nuances with their children that they would with the necessary contact time, and if they were being more vigilant. We often do not detect the emergence of things negative, for we'd like to believe that our children are simply normal and that they are not likely to go "off the rails" and do horrible things. We are most often in denial and a typical refrain that we use erroneously is "not my child."

A serious misjudgment that I made with John was not recognizing that he was probably a teen alcoholic. There were a number of indications that I did not pick up on: his practice of taking the hinges off of my locked bar and siphoning off levels of drinks and bringing the bottles back up to level by adding water. His two serious auto accidents under suspicious circumstances, one in which he rammed his car into the side of a neighbor's house, narrowly missing a young boy sleeping in his bedroom; the other colliding with a couple in a Karmann Ghia and injuring the female passenger. But there was another incident, which had the direst of consequences and which will be shared later. John was my staunchest supporter and had uncommon insight, for a child, into the nature of the conflict that ravaged our family.

My third son, Gerald, was the middle child, which, according to theories on birth order, very frequently gets lost in the shuffle. He was kind of non-descript, kept a pretty low profile and seemed to be dragged along in the wake of his older brothers. Gerald had serious attention deficit problems, so performance for him was never above average and most often tended to be substandard. He was mannerly, always respectful but was suggestible and too easily led by irrational suggestions. He was apt to follow the path of least resistance, which often meant avoiding run-of-the-mill responsibilities. In an effort to get him up to his chronological performance level, I once convinced his mother to have him come to live with me and attend school in our area so that I could monitor his progress and get the necessary medical and psychological help that he obviously needed. All was in place and he was doing quite well when his mother, without warning, came to the community school, withdrew him, and took him back to Santa Ana. Everything seemed to go even farther downhill for him from that point on.

Gerald had led a troubled life, having problems in school, which spilled over into other aspects of his life. He never was able to exhibit a sense of responsibility, having fathered a son, Psalm David, to whom he showed little regard. Maybe he could be forgiven for his inattention to his son because of his own problem, but I was not capable of understanding why parental instinct did not kick in. The *blue skies* are that Psalmy and his wife, Lorena, presented me with three lovely and exceptionally bright great granddaughters, Sadie, Alexya, and Milanya, whom I do see and would love to see more often.

My fourth son, Reggie, probably came along at an opportune stage of his development, for he appeared not to be too devastated by the new order of things. He had always been extraordinarily athletic, which kept him focused on being as good as his talents would make him. From junior high school he was perceived as a comer. Coaches at two universities were already tracking him with the notion that some day he would play for them. This worked out as he transferred from community college and played baseball at UCLA (on a full scholarship) for one of the coaches who had been watching him and had now taken over the Bruin program. He left UCLA in his senior year and from there, he was drafted by the California Angels organization and moved up to their triple A team in Edmonton, Alberta, Canada, where he played for a few years (one step away from the "Big Dance" in Anaheim). He eventually gave it up and returned to Southern California where he now resides.

While at UCLA, Reggie was involved with a young lady and, apparently, was unable to remember why he was there. I knew that he was in trouble as we checked him into a co-ed dorm and witnessed young ladies in baby-doll pajamas leaning over face basins brushing their teeth. Focus didn't come too easily when it seemed that there were better options than academics, such as women. And so he then succumbed to the draft in his senior year and went off to seek riches. Here emerges a major lesson for young dreamers. By now we knew all too well what being a prospective professional athlete was all about. Of course, there is the fantasy regarding big money and all that goes along with it. For too many of our young men, the driving motivation is to acquire an elaborate house and amenities for their mothers. And it doesn't help if the mothers' aspirations are the same. The proverbial "meal ticket." And while it all seems noble and selfless on the young athletes' part, the truth is that very few of those who have such aspirations will achieve their goals. It then becomes necessary to keep both feet on the ground and to consider the "what ifs." Accordingly, my emphatic advice was, and continues to be, "As you move along in your athletic career, never forget to bring your education along. There is a very good chance that you'll outlive your athleticism. Then what?" There is a reason for everything, and Reggie is a totally dedicated father to his four children. (He once threatened to have twelve. But time and experience with those he already has have taught him a lesson. I think.) And he stays in touch, which I really appreciate. I am very proud of him.

There are two qualities that I have hoped to pass on to my children: a strong work ethic and an unflinching dedication to their children. For most of them it has worked. Reggie, for example, has four children and a granddaughter, and the unbelievable number of hours he puts in at his job is for the sole purpose of providing for their needs. It would not occur to anyone who knows him that he would have any other priority.

On the other hand, Ronnie, though committed to hard and sustained work, was devoted only to the children he happened to be with at the time. He was married three times, producing four children. I never forgave him for what can only be labeled abandonment of his first two daughters from his first marriages, Andrea, who is a real doer and who stays in touch with me, and Miriam, who is not and does not. And it is unimaginable to me that he never had any contact with his beautiful and very bright granddaughter, Brianna (my oldest great grandchild, who is excelling in high school and is currently visiting college campuses for next year), and his only grandson, Raymond.

Ronnie had a tough adult life. Maybe the negative potential was always there, but it seems to me that everything came apart at the seams after the divorce. I continually wrestle with the question of impact. Would the lives of the children have been different if I had remained in an untenable situation with Juliet? I generally do not get beyond the only answer possible, that there was no way possible that I could have stayed with it and maintained my sanity. Without that sanity, I would not have been of value to anyone. I am quite aware that children are the emotional debris of divorce. The best that I was capable of doing at that point was to work as hard as I could to assure all of the children, especially Ronnie, who seemed to be most affected, that I would always be there for them, and actually not too far away. That assurance was far less effective with Ronnie than the others. Thus began a series of tragedies that would be virtually unparalleled in the annals of family history.

23

THE DOWNWARD SPIRAL

It all began one evening as Suzanne and I were visiting with my friend, George Woods, and his wife in our home in Anaheim when I received a call from the recreation center at Jerome Park in Santa Ana. The call was from the director who frantically reported that Ronnie had shot a boy with whom I was familiar from pick-up football games in the park. As I arrived at the center, I learned that the boy had died and that Ronnie had disappeared. It was said that the police were looking for him, and my first thoughts were that he would be found and harmed. I went to the police station in the hopes that he would be brought in unharmed. After some very anxious moments he was escorted into the station and booked. That was the first and perhaps the most important hurdle. It was a double tragedy, for I felt almost as strongly about the boy's family's loss as I did about what would now happen to Ronnie. At least he was alive. Any future that he might have had was now all but ruined. As a parent, it was rough sitting in court watching the proceedings. It was equally painful to visit the three institutions at which he was confined, including San Quentin. There were no really *blue skies* here, except that now when I discuss deviance, especially crime and punishment, my perception is not theoretical.

Although the causes of crime elude me, from Ronnie's point of view the deed was justified and needed to be done. It seems that the boy, who was a couple of years older than John, was physically abusing John and refused to stop when Ronnie asked him to. Ronnie went home, returned with a gun and shot him. He saw himself as the protector who was responsible for John's safety. There had to be a better way. Was it about fear, or anger, or family pride, or a defensive mode that went too far? Obviously, consequences were not a consideration, which brings into question the issue of punishment being a deterrent to crime. Because of the other young man's jaded reputation with drug dealing activities in the community, Ronnie's sentence was relatively light. But the incarceration experience did not serve him well, for in spite of the party line about the purpose of imprisonment, prisons are now recognized, by anyone who pays attention, as academies for crime. I learned when talking with guards at San Quentin, that you can forget the spiel about rehabilitation. Their job, they say, is to isolate them and protect the good people in society. Being a model prisoner, he was released in a rather short period of time. Apparently, making adjustment to his newfound freedom did not go too smoothly. He wound up on the streets, and when his mother located him, he was in extremely poor health. He got the medical attention that he needed and was up and running again. He was able to get good jobs somehow and, true to form, was considered a valued employee. He felt the need to get a fresh start and came to stay with us in Mission Viejo for a while. He saw an ad in the newspaper for a metal processor position, for which he was very qualified. The company was in the Bay Area, which seemed a little far-fetched to me. But he felt confident and had my daughter, Semara, type a letter of application for him. It was sent and, lo and behold, he received a phone call from the company inviting him to come up, at their expense, for an interview. By the time he returned home, he received another call from the company offering him the job.

I bought him a very nice automobile from a close friend, Nat Dyer, staked him with money for housing and other living expenses and bade him farewell, with a serious warning: stay away from the seedier parts of Oakland. I suppose it was only a matter of time before the lure became too great and he gave in, probably believing he could handle it. I knew Oakland from my days in San Francisco and was familiar with its dangers. However, Oakland can't be blamed for the choices Ronnie made, especially with regards to his choice of a third marital partner. She was really bad news, even for Ronnie and his history. He fathered his third and fourth children with her–both daughters. He brought them down to visit with us. Although I am not a prude by a long shot, I could not believe his wife's lack of class and decorum. I especially felt sorry for the cute little girls who would be reared in their mother's presence. Ronnie actually talked with me about the relationship and attributed her appeal solely to sex. Tragically, most of my sons have fallen into the same trap as their father in his first marriage. I don't know how many times I heard from them "It's only about sex." In fact, I don't believe it was only about sex in all cases. I think that it was mostly about bluster and chest-beating. At any rate, this one was so crude and obnoxious that I had to ask Ronnie not to bring her to our home again, which was difficult because on a certain level he had to have had some kind of commitment to her. Drugs were a part of her lifestyle, and it made sense to me that this was something else that they shared in common. That lifestyle cost him his life. On December 22, 1995, I received a phone call from my daughter, Terri, reporting that Ronnie had died of an overdose of heroine. This was the last (hopefully) of six late night horrifying phone calls that I would receive over the years.

The first loss, of course, was Tracy Lomax, the young man that Ronnie shot and killed. The pain that had to be felt by his family for a child who never reached adulthood had to be unbearable, as I would later experience myself. The second and most excruciatingly painful for me personally was the death of John, Jr., at the age of 27 in 1980. Again, it was a late night call from his mother announcing that he had been in an auto accident and was in the hospital in Fountain Valley. I am not a strong believer in premonition, but as I drove from Anaheim to Fountain Valley, I had the sense that we had lost him. Sure enough, when I arrived, he had been pronounced dead. Heart wrenching. It is said that the greatest loss a parent can experience is the loss of a child. Twenty-nine years have passed, and I still have not fully recovered from that loss. The questions never stop. I have grown to be smart enough to not expect any answers, but not smart enough to stop asking them. Why? Why does a young man with tons of potential get prevented from experiencing his thirties and forties and fifties, ad infinitum? Why not take an old codger like me who has been to the mountaintop? What is my purpose for being? Why take a totally dedicated father who had an inseparable relationship with his son, John III, who would miss him dearly? There are probably some answers out there beyond cyberspace, but by now I understand them to be irretrievable.

John never failed to visit with me on weekends, always with John III (John-John) in tow. He drove a little Triumph sports car with the top down, which nearly drove me insane. I complained about the danger to him and John-John, but he simply blew my concerns off, assuring me that all would be fine. It was the car in which he died in a one-car accident. His roommate was with him, and I was thankful that he was only slightly injured. I was even more thankful that John-John was not with him.

John was extraordinarily intelligent and seemed to be far beyond his chronological age. I had often wondered how he could be so bright at his young age and had a difficult time visualizing him as an older adult. As it turned out, I would never have that pleasure. He floundered a bit after the divorce, but not so much so as to lose sight of rationality. He had John-John with a girlfriend, who happened to be the sister of his first girlfriend. He was wrested away from the older and classier one by the younger one's charms, which was one of those wrong turns in the road for him. John-John was exposed to constant danger in his environment. There was a great deal of gang activity in Westminster where he lived and attended school. On one occasion he was stabbed in the chest by some gang members, narrowly missing his heart. He realized what he was up against and asked if he could come to Mission Viejo and live with us. We were delighted that we could help to get him out of that environment, realizing that violence can reside anywhere, even in South Orange County.

John-John was the same age as our youngest children, the twins, Tia and Josh. He was enrolled at their high school, Capistrano Valley, was a member of the football team and was doing quite well. Our problems began when he asked that I be responsible for his social security allowance. At this point, his mother wanted him back with her. She went so far as to bring his girlfriend to his practice field to persuade him to go back to Westminster. I suppose a young man has to have a tremendous amount of resolve to resist that kind of temptation, and he soon decided to leave.

It was not too long before I received the dreaded telephone call from his uncle saying that John-John had been shot and was in the hospital. When I arrived in Orange at the hospital, he was on life support. He died a couple of days later. It seems that he and a couple of his friends were hanging out at one of their apartments, without parental supervision. There was horseplay with a revolver and as John-John was sitting on a sofa eating chocolate ice cream, a younger quick-draw artist had the firearm go off and strike him in the head. To show the kind of people we were dealing with here, they were selling tee shirts emblazoned with his picture at his services. Another good place for "what ifs." We are still in touch with the first sister that John dated. She is a gem, an elementary school teacher, and for John Jr., a missed opportunity.

In 1987, I had received yet another awful call, this time as well from Terri, who was with her mother. This time it was Gerald, my third son, who had died of injuries incurred in a domestic accident. He had attempted to get into their second story window and fell from a ledge, causing him to be mortally injured. At this point, in addition to the loss, I am beginning to wonder not only about the succession of deaths, but also about the long-term effect on my young daughter, Terri, who was continually observing and reporting the decimation of our family.

In 1988, Mama died of a stroke. She always said that she'd go that way. Hers was the only death that seemed almost normal. She was 78, much too young, from my perspective, but it was pretty clear that she was ready. I would hope that it was because she had lived a full, active, though sometimes troubled life and, apparently, had no qualms about her own impending death. Other possible reasons for her being ready, though, are somewhat bothersome. Could it be that life was no longer something to be enthusiastic about, so no need to stick around? Or had her journey been so unpleasant that death was a better alternative? She had mentioned at the deaths of John and Gerald that it was not natural for parents to survive their children. Was she wondering who would be next?

Mama was frighteningly practical and self sufficient to the point of being stubborn. Bay-Suh and I were concerned primarily because after my stepfather's death in Birmingham, she moved to Los Angeles and absolutely insisted on having her own place. In fact, my wife and I had purchased a larger home, anticipating that she would be receptive to living with us. We had visions of something horrible happening to her in her neat little home in the Wilshire District and no one would know of her demise for too long a time. But in keeping with her penchant for control, it happened just the way she would have orchestrated it. We all called often, especially Bay-Suh, who also lived in Los Angeles and Lil' Miriam, Bay-Suh's daughter. On one occasion Lil' Miriam called her and detected a slur in her voice. She insisted on going over to see about her and get her to the hospital if necessary. When she arrived, Lil' Miriam found Mama sitting calmly reading, dressed and ready to go. She had laid out her papers and instructions for Bay-Suh and me, handwritten. "First, I want to be cremated. There is money here—money there to cover expenses. This goes to this one. That, to that one, etc. Sell the house in Birmingham." Bay-Suh and I followed her instructions to the letter. We knew better than to do otherwise.

That wonderful little woman could not have imagined the influence that would emanate from such a physically modest being. It is not surprising that her descendants, almost to a person, have perceived her to be the imposing matriarch. Her wisdom shone through with every utterance. Her ever-present college degree that hung on the most wretched walls in the most forsaken communities continues to inspire us all. It is often said that parents who go to college are likely to have children who go to college. With limited exceptions, that theory has withstood the test of time. The theory pulled me out of twelve years of Marine Corps life. It was not easy being a thirty-one year-old freshman, but because of Mama's influence, it was better than the alternative. Perhaps most important is the exponential impact felt by her grandchildren and the long-term influence to accrue over the generations. I recall an old black-and-white movie that I was watching recently where a statement was made to the effect that "You are not dead until you are forgotten." Long live Mama.

By now, I have been so traumatized by late night emergency calls that any call after nine o'clock in the evening is cause for alarm. The downside of producing such a large family is that you always wonder when the other shoe will drop. As with many other responsible parents, when alarms or emergency sirens go off, you immediately stop, count heads, and wonder about those not living in your household.

It would be a glorious gift if we could put the deaths of family members behind us and simply say, "enough already." But that is not the way of life, and the most that we may hope for is that future losses will result from "natural" causes, whatever that means. You could argue that dying in a Triumph sports car accident, falling from a second-story ledge, being shot in the head accidentally, and dying from an overdose of drugs are all natural phenomena. And that disease, warfare and catastrophic tragedies all amount to natural causes. We might argue that it is all about the natural weeding-out process necessary to curtail human population growth. But emotions typically will not allow us to accept this rationale at face value. We want answers that comfort us, God, and we want them now. Rationalize, hypothesize, theorize, and criticize all you choose, but don't hold your breath.

I have very often been asked how I manage to maintain sanity in light of the unbelievable losses that I have endured. I think that, in large part, Mama had subtly, and maybe without intent, prepared me to accept the reality of life and death. "You're not promised tomorrow" was a frequent refrain. You learn to view life in waves or generations of humanity. You get your allotted time on earth and you make the most of it. Some people's allotted time is much shorter than others, and I have witnessed phenomenal amounts of life squeezed into very short life spans for some people. An excellent example is my former urologist, Mark Sullivan, who was as amazing as anyone I've ever known, not only as a renowned surgeon, but also because of his eclectic lifestyle. He was an inventor, an author, and raised prized orchids and roses. He was a rare coin collector and held membership in two societies of magicians. He died of complications from diabetes. He was 58 years old. By all accounts, it was a full 58 years. But a more profound example was Dr. Martin Luther King, Jr., who was only 39 when he was assassinated. How much history of and influence on society had been pounded into the 39 years of his short life?

I ascribe my own survival skills in the face of my children's deaths to several things: One, no matter how devastating the loss, nothing you do or say is going to change the course of events. Two, no matter how many you lose, there are those left who need you, and you can't give to others what you do not have. Three, Elisabeth Kubler-Ross's five stages of death and dying make some kind of sense, though taken to task by many other theorists. Those stages are denial, anger, negotiation, depression, and acceptance. She insists that people go though all five stages exactly as listed if they are to deal with death successfully and that the same rules apply to the impending death of a loved one as with one's own impending death. She further asserts that the same rules apply to other serious losses, such as divorce. The problem with psychologist Kubler-Ross was that when she died in 2004, she did not adhere to her own exhortations. She lamented the fact that too many people never get past the first two stages. She, herself, never got past the anger stage. The goal is to go through them all until reaching acceptance. On the several occasions of my personal losses, I experienced all but the negotiation stage. I think that I understood that I had no bargaining chips.

People who have had to go through seriously rough times seem better equipped to pick up the pieces and move on when things do not go as desired, provided they do not go under from the experience. The ordeal is likely to either subdue you or make you stronger. I feel that I am definitely stronger as a result of the several blows I've taken. Each blow got a little easier to take. Defense mechanisms take over, and you become more and more fortified for the next hit. I've had enough fortification now, thank you, and I wonder if it is possible to take one too many such losses and reach the breaking point. Is there such a thing as "loss build-up"?

It is said that life is for the living, as long as we don't for a moment forget the spirit of those who have gone on before us. Leo Buscaglia has said, "None of us will get out of this world alive." The day-to-day emphasis must be placed on the demands our living loved ones and we continually face. There are inevitably negative aspects of our lives, but we must never forget the *blue skies*. The beauty in life far outweighs the ugliness. It is interesting that we focus more on the negatives, much like small children who learn to say "No!" and "Mine!" much sooner than "Yes" and "Ours."

24

. . . And the Spiral Upward

I am extremely thankful for the existence of the family members who are still with us and thriving well. In addition to my two children from my first marriage, Reggie and Terri, Suzanne and I have three children: Semara, Tia, and Josh. As much as anything else, I appreciate the relationships they have all formed with one another. As we parents grow older, we become more and more concerned about the well-being of our children, even older adult children. The question becomes, "Have I done my job? Have I adequately prepared the children to be independent and self-sufficient in my absence?" For the most part, the answer that I get is a resounding "Yes." But the "Yes" did not come easily. And, of course, there is always room for self-doubt on the part of parents, as we wonder if children would have turned out just fine anyway, even without our influence. But we dare not take the chance.

Terri, my oldest daughter and born to my first wife, has exhibited extraordinary strength of character through tumultuous times. She did it all while displaying amazing loyalty to her mother, who was taking her through some challenging experiences. I continually reminded her to maintain that loyalty and not to feel obligated to choose sides in our divorce, a situation not of her making. I sensed that she had already made that decision and what I had to say would only serve to reinforce her stance.

When we divorced, I was made responsible for any remaining bills, including the unworn expensive clothing that Juliet had amassed, and for the mortgage payment. In addition to treating my children as her own, my wife, Sue, helped me out of a serious financial hole at the outset. I came to her battered by an uninformed court decree. That initial support from her is what made all that followed possible, including my schooling. I had never known what it was like to pursue my goals unencumbered. I had left a decent four-bedroom home in Santa Ana where the children were assured of the shelter to which they had become accustomed. When the children were living with me in Anaheim and Lake Forest for what seemed like an indefinite period of time, I ceased to send their mother child support payments. My position was that the money follows the children. But I didn't make that change through the courts, and so she came after me with threats of court action, which I really didn't want and could avoid with what seemed at the time to be an unfair compromise. She wanted the home all to herself. The agreement and court order stipulated that I would be responsible for a mortgage that was in both of our names, and that when and if we sold it, we were to split the proceeds. That wasn't enough for her, so I agreed to quit claim the place to her, which would get my name off of a document that I did not feel comfortable sharing with her anyway.

The first mistake she made was to secure a second mortgage, which she couldn't pay, then more loans with the same result. Soon the home was in foreclosure, and she, and by now only Terri, were out. I was concerned for Terri and sought to find out where they were. The logical place would have been with some of her folks in Los Angeles. What I learned instead was that they were in some dive in the downtown area. I drove up to see if I could find them and by some fluke found them in a flop-house in skid row, where I had to step over the drunks and homeless people sleeping in doorways. Terri has given accounts of how awful it was to have to take the bus to Hamilton High School where she was afraid to make friends, for she didn't want students to know where she lived. She was on the tennis team, as she had been at Santa Ana Valley High School. So, at the end of the school day, she would quietly pack up her tennis gear and board the bus for "home," not wanting her schoolmates to know what her situation was.

She graduated from Hamilton High and asked if she could come to live with us to attend Saddleback College. That worked out well and then we had four teenagers in the home. I think that was where the bonding first occurred. Terri majored in journalism at Saddleback, graduated and was eventually married in Los Angeles. She later attended California State University, Northridge, where she graduated with a degree in journalism. She has been executive producer of the "McIntyre in the Morning" radio talk show (790 KABC on your radio dial).

I can't say enough about Terri's resolve and fortitude. She has expressed to me her determination to be a successful, productive woman. I see some of Mama in all of my daughters. My mother felt a special affinity for Terri, for she sensed her resolve against debilitating odds. Needless to say, Mama was not a wealthy woman. But when she died, she favored Terri as her financial resources were distributed among the grandchildren. She knew that Terri would be more in need than any of the others. On the lighter side, Terri is a devout *I Love Lucy* fan, as evidenced by memorabilia throughout her apartment. She once talked of being a stand-up comic. She can be very funny.

Terri's running buddy and "roomie" when she lived with us was Semara, the oldest of the three children of my marriage to Sue. Semara had natural intellectual ability. She scored in the genius range on I.Q. tests, but she chose not to put that talent to work until the later stages of young adulthood. A basic tenet in learning theory says that you perform best when you understand and appreciate what you learn and when you know how information is to be used. Family, including three wonderful children and a husband to die for, brought it all into focus. She did nothing in high school and later everything that she touched at university turned into "A's." In fact, she was recently initiated into the Honor Society of Phi Kappa Phi at Cal State University at Fullerton. A long way from walking off from courses at Saddleback without officially dropping, which resulted in a long list of "F"s. One of her problems as a child was her deviant nature. (Where'd she get *that* from?) She used to complain about the sterility of Mission Viejo where we lived, in favor of the "streets" where she was involved in a little bit of everything dangerous. I cringe when the adult children share with me some of the things they did as adolescents. They sought out areas where there were drive-bys, because it was exciting. I learned very early on, though, to never utter the words "not my children." We'd like to believe that ours have been brought up properly and would stay within the boundaries of decency. But decency, at that age, can be boring. And most of our children, all of us, will do whatever their peers will do, whether we like it or believe it or not. Sometimes it is best not to know what is going on with them, for we probably could not take it.

Semara had a grown-up attitude even as a pre-teen. Adult women liked having earnest conversations with her on what seemed like an equal level. Her range of intelligence presented unforeseen problems as well. It was tough to confine her to responsibilities commensurate with her chronological age. She needed to function outside of the box. Her attitude kept her in trouble in school. She refused to turn in homework. Her room would get to be so messy that we wondered what might be growing in there and could no longer simply close the door and let it fester. So we'd feel compelled to go in on occasion and clean it up. We would find completed homework stuffed between her mattress and box springs, and when we'd ask why she didn't turn it in, she'd reply that she had done the work and saw no reason to have to prove anything to anyone. In my deviant little head, I kind of liked that thinking (secretly), but I shuttered to think of the point being missed about how life works. It took her family, Shea, Stevan, Spencer, and Sean (Dad) Simon (note the "S" theme) to turn up the heat. She is now on fire.

I have thought that a part of Semara's obstinacy about school was because of her displeasure with being moved from El Toro High School to Capistrano Valley High when we moved. But then I remembered that her delinquency began at El Toro High where she was the number one singles tennis player on the varsity team as a freshman. We got reports of suspicious activities involving Semara in the tarp shed near the athletic field. The suspicions were confirmed; thus, began some concern about her inclinations. I had been warned by her first tennis instructor in Anaheim a few years earlier that "you'd better keep an eye on Semara." This female coach had noticed that Semara was kind of aggressive with the boys. Semara liked boys.

The last of my children were twins, Tia and Josh. Having fathered six children already, I resisted having any more after Semara. But my wife, Sue, insisted that Semara needed companionship and that we should go for one more. Oops! What was meant to be one turned out to be two, and I was shamefully and painfully unhappy initially. I felt inundated with children and thought that there were already enough to properly provide for. It was already a stretch. But what started out to be displeasure evolved into a new and exciting experience. We did the Lamaze method, a good way to get fathers into the mix (if they don't faint). Tia came first and continues to lord the fact over Josh's head. Josh was a footling breach and didn't arrive for about fifty-five minutes after Tia; therefore, Tia is "older." It was both humorous and frustrating for all concerned as he lay in repose with one leg hanging out. Sue remarked that it could only be a boy who would cause so much trouble. We made every attempt to ensure that the twins were regarded and treated as individuals, and they developed as such. In the early years Josh showed compassion and concern for his sister. If good fortune came his way in the form of goodies or gifts, he would always ask, "What about Tia?" We thought that was cute and in keeping with what is to be expected of twins. Tia, on the other hand, was aloof and showed little regard for Josh. As they grew into the teens, they vowed that they would never like each other, which was disheartening to us as we envisioned them as adults. Fortunately, they first came to relate to each other in young adulthood, and now they have become close friends. Ironically, the tables slowly turned and Tia became the concerned one who seeks to maintain contact and to inquire about issues in his life.

Their experiences in high school were somewhat similar to those of Bay-Suh's and mine. Bay-Suh was the social one and also the academic achiever. Though two years younger than I, her standards were the yardstick by which I was judged. Tia's talent lay in her tenacity and a sense of knowing what needed to be done and then getting it done. Being a community college educator, I tried to convince her of the merits of a community college education: the cost factor, the convenience, the smaller classes, and what I believe to be better undergraduate education. But her acquaintances were all university bound, and for many of them there was stigma attached to "junior" college. Having gone through all the segments of higher education, I am quick to inform anyone who will listen that we are not "junior" to anyone and that three or four units of credit from our institutions will compare favorably with those from Harvard, Yale, USC, Stanford, or anyone else who chooses to play the game. No amount of my discourse would convince her, though. So off to U.C. Santa Barbara she went. I am certain that a group of her friends had already envisioned themselves at Isla Vista for the reputed non-stop partying. Of course, I had serious concerns about her ability to focus on her real purpose for being there. She did a better job of convincing me than I had done in convincing her. She said that she knew where the line was drawn and would get the work done. I wished her well and indicated that I saw having fun to be a large part of the college experience. Funny, but I believed that she knew what she was doing.

She majored in Sociology and Anthropology (what a novel concept) and felt after two years at UCSB that she really wanted to graduate from UCLA. So she transferred, graduating from UCLA in 1998 with Honors (Cum Laude) with the B.A. in Sociology and a minor in Anthropology. She then enrolled in law school at the University of Southern California, graduating in 2001 with the Juris Doctorate. But wait. On the way there, she and her then boyfriend (now husband) sat in our living room and told me that they were pregnant. I said a few damns and other choice words and then settled down enough to realize intellectually that it was a matter of where we go from here. I was more than visibly upset until Tia assured me that she would finish law school on schedule. Once again, I believed her and once again she did not disappoint me.

Just four years prior to Tia's revelations about her pregnancy, I had sat in our same living room with Semara and Sean to receive the same message. I remained cool enough to offer them to come to live with us for one year, and they would pay us an apartment's worth of rent. At the end of the year I would give them all of the money that they had paid to be used as a down payment for their first home, which they purchased in Lake Forest. There has never been a single day in their thirteen years of marriage that I have not marveled at the beauty of their relationship.

Tia, who has practiced law at a firm in Newport Beach, and another in Central Orange County, is currently teaching a college Marriage and Family course. She has fared equally well in her marriage of seven years to Carlo Grasso. Carlo taught middle school and has recently become a vice principal in the Irvine Unified School District. He received his B.A. and M.A. from UCLA, where he and Tia met. Imagine where the lines are drawn in their home when it involves USC versus UCLA, though I sense that Tia doesn't really care one way or the other, having graduated from both. Carlo, though, is blue and gold. I have said frequently that no one could have finer sons-in-law than the two we are blessed with. And to top it off, they are very close friends with each other. They both meet a basic criterion that is shared enthusiastically in our family. They are both exceptional parents.

The last and youngest (by 55 minutes) is my son, Josh. Very frankly, when I have agonized over whether or not we had done a decent job of getting the children to be ready to be on their own, Josh was my main concern. I wondered if he'd ever be ready to be organized and responsible. I have been relieved over the last few years as he turned the corner and headed in the right direction. For a number of years he was "finding himself." A key factor in his turn-around has been his marriage to Sarah King, a wonderful and loyal daughter-in-law who, in addition to being a great mother, has done a good job of helping to "settle him down." (See cp-16, #1). I could never imagine him focusing well enough to hold any kind of job years ago. And he did flounder as I did in adolescence. Jobs were short lived. Attention was short. But time is an excellent healer, and for eight years he has worked in medical management doing pre-certification for surgery and insurance coverage. He is currently Billing Coordinator for a company that he has been with for a number of years. Josh, too, had done some wild things. Some years ago he traveled to the Northwest with "friends" where he got stranded and panhandled in Washington State. In a phone conversation with him, I detected that he was in desperate straits and offered to wire him money for a plane trip home. He did not hesitate for a moment to accept the offer. When I met him at the airport, he smelled to high heaven and I felt pity for the person who had to sit next to him on the plane. He has cleaned up nicely and has made me proud of him as a responsible father and husband.

While all of the children were good tennis players and Semara had the purest game, I think that Josh had the most long-term potential. He had the makings of a young Pete Sampras and reminded me of him as I watched him play tournaments. But he got sidetracked because most of the boys that he associated with did not play tennis. They played pick-up hoops and video games, and Josh allowed himself to be lured away from a talent that could have paid him dividends for a lifetime.

It was not uncommon during my young adulthood for families to have too many children, although my total of eight were far beyond reason, even for that period. Needless to say, not an awful lot of family planning went into the thought processes of the day. In fact, there were no thought processes at all. Today, families have about 1.8 children per family, not enough, really, to replenish our population. Some of the reasons for this decrease include concern for world population growth, more pervasive use of sophisticated contraception, especially the pill, a larger percentage of women in the workforce, and more women pursuing higher education. But perhaps the dominant reason has to do with economics. Some accounts insist that it takes about $300,000 to rear a child from birth to eighteen. Some say that it takes three times the household's annual income. The government, which tends to lowball such estimates, comes up with a figure of about $160,000 for middle-income family. Remember, all of these estimates do not cover college costs. So parents, wisely, have figured with very basic math that two or more children can be an extremely costly enterprise. Without college. In my Marriage and Family classes I plead with students, as parents, to hold something back for themselves. Resources are required for parents to recreate and regroup, which are necessary in order to do good parenting.

Although I was not bright enough to refrain from having too many children and had the depressing experience of losing three of them, there are indeed *blue skies* for which to be grateful. I have five remaining wonderful children who help to give my life purpose. Even at this late date, Sue and I continue to parent, she in her way and I in mine. And with eighteen grandchildren (the nineteenth on the way) and five great grandchildren, there's no end in sight for parenting.

25

WORK AND ME, THE ADULT BRAND

And then comes my work. Too much of our self-concept is related to our jobs—especially for males. We define our worth using our occupations as the yardstick. Our work, then, dominates our existence. No meaningful work, no worth. I was reminded of this tragically a few years ago when a very dear friend decided that, because he had been out of work for about three years, his life was not worth living. So, he ended it. This was a man with whom I had played tennis every Friday at one o'clock for almost ten years, without fail. Having done responsible and lucrative work in his lifetime, he was not willing to settle for less. In his farewell note to me, he lamented the notion that at the age of sixty, no potential employer would be interested in talking with him. No work, no worth. Never mind the devastation and agony that he left in his wake with a loving and adoring family.

Since this tragic incident occurred at the height of a severe recession, I wondered how many other men decided to end it all because, due to downsizing and outsourcing, many people who lost jobs in mid-life would never go to work again. I am convinced that there was more suicide than was recorded during that period. Disturbingly, currently we appear to be headed into a deeper recession and, based on past experience, shouldn't we keep an eye on issues such as depression as it impacts people who have always been employed and self-sufficient? Why should an employer recall workers at the peak of their earning capacity when they could get two or three entry- level workers for the same money? Industry did learn, however, that it was not necessarily cost-effective to get rid of older workers via golden handshakes, since they were also getting rid of valuable experience and just as valuable communication skills. So many older workers have been called up again to come back, on their own terms, as consultants.

Society and the Transmission of Knowledge

I thrive on work. And I think that earlier on (after my flaky youth) I took it much too seriously and tied too much of me to my work. Although I still see work to be more than simply a means to an end, I feel fortunate now that I can put it into proper perspective. Do good work. Be satisfied at the end of the day that you have accomplished something significant. That means, in my profession, that you have opened some doors to new knowledge for the students that you encounter each day, even if only a handful of them, in spite of the fact that many come to you thinking that they already know it all. I find it interesting that this already-know-it-all attitude is not unique to the young. I distinctly remember entering college as an older adult feeling that my life experiences probably superseded those of some of the young whip-persnappers who taught my courses. Surprise. What I knew was good and useful. But it was not all that I needed to know in order to be a well-rounded human being. Needless to say, I encounter a bit of that in a few of the more chronologically mature students in my classes. I try to exercise patience, re-alizing that as time passes they are likely to lighten up, settle down, and see our relationship as symbiotic. Leo Buscaglia says "If you live to be a hundred and nine, be willing to be open to new information tomorrow."

The business of higher education is, by its very nature, bureaucratic. I try to get across to students that our tendency to feel negatively about bureaucra-cies is a mistake. With the size and complexity of our society, it would be impossible to get our necessary functions accomplished without bureaucracy. Granted, our interactions with them are not always pleasant. But we could not function out of Mom and Pop operations. So it becomes a matter of as-suming the proper mind-set when dealing with them. I am convinced that the proper preparation makes almost anything bearable, including death. My first thirty-nine years in higher education would put all of my convictions to the test. I wish I had started my preparation a lot sooner, for among all the wonderfully positive things that transpired in my career, there would also be unbelievable ugliness.

I have come to find what I see to be a principle purpose in my life. At the risk of seeming more gracious or compassionate than I really am, I have become obsessed with sharing with young folks what I finally know about life. And this is not an ego trip, for I am not so certain that my experiences will work well in combination with others' experiences. I am certain that for some the only way to the truth is through self. The smarter ones (or the more gullible ones) will listen and maybe benefit from both the good and the bad of others' lives. When I am dispensing what I think are gems of wisdom to a class of about fifty students, or nineteen or twenty in honors classes, success for me is getting through to maybe three or four who will hear and remember. There is no greater joy than to receive positive feedback from them, especially after considerable time has lapsed. It is essential that young people, too, get the feel of the ever-present *blue skies*.

As I view the totality of the life course, I see it all coming together to form the unique individual. As with culture, it is the sum of all the parts that cre-ates the whole. So, we are all the products of all that we have experienced, which explains, in addition to biology, why no two individuals are identical. Looking at the various aspects of life that are so much a part of our daily lives, some are critical and stand out at every turn. They are the following: 1. education, 2. bureaucracy, 3. politics, 4. the family, 5. sex and gender, and 6. religion, not necessarily in that order. The emphasis in my classes very often deals with the inequities in all six of these areas.

I feel safe in saying that education is the surest pathway to success. This does not mean that education is a get-rich-quick scheme. And it does not mean that those with the paperwork are necessarily the brightest of the lot. What it does mean is that those who are credentialed have persisted in pursuing their goals. Very often they leave it all in the ivory towers and feel that they have done all they need to do. But the combination of integrity, common sense, street smarts, a strong work ethic, and formal education are what make for success. None of these five alone will get the job done over the long term.

My own track record with education has been checkered at best, beginning with my smart-alecky performance in high school. After managing to squeak out of high school with what I think was the lowest possible grade point average (I also think that in my own mind, I have exaggerated how bad I really was), I was away in the Marines removed from anything that resembled civilian educational processes for thirteen years. I have not, however, devalued the education I was receiving during the military years, both in interpersonal relationships and in the world of work. Education is the sum of *all* of life's experiences. It doesn't all happen in the classroom. In fact, I think that it is because of the combination of formal and informal education that my understanding and perceptions have been broadened to include much of what is going on in my world. Another rough spot in my education occurred when I was dealing with my divorce: I was asked to leave the university on academic probation. After getting out of the service with just a little bit of doubt because of my horrible high school performance and my successes in the Marine Corps, I was running scared and, consequently, doing very well academically. The dismissal from university experience could have spelled the end of my dreams if I had been just a little weaker. Actually, it was a blessing in disguise because I was convinced that nothing could stop people but themselves. There is no defined limit to human potential, a message students in my classes are likely to hear over and over again.

My exasperations with education are many. Probably my biggest frustration is how this society has treated the institution. Citizens are more apt to throw rocks at schools and accuse them of not properly educating their children than to become supportive and involved in the process. They often forget what made most successful people successful, although everyone cannot be a

Bill Gates, who left Harvard as a junior. My county has a national reputation for not passing educational bond issues. The few that have passed recently were aberrations. While it is absolutely true that you cannot solve problems by simply throwing money at them, it is also true that you get what you pay for. In my thirty-nine year California Community College career, I have witnessed the decimation of the system's ability to deliver its product to an alarming degree, beginning with Proposition 13, passed by California voters in 1978 to reduce property taxes by 57%. And while on the surface there appeared to be an upsurge in the state's economy, you have to wonder how that plays out by castigating the premier community college on the surface of the earth. Ultimately, who will pay the price? And it has to be about more than immediate gratification and what you'll save on your next tax bill. The bill will be hundreds of times higher over the long term as a result of the loss of human resources. I am confounded by the shortsightedness of those who already have theirs and who are not concerned about those who are hurting. For purely selfish reasons it seems to me that it benefits all to live in an educated society. The higher the society's educational level, the higher the mean earning capacity. I love that now popular slogan, "If you think education is expensive, try ignorance."

I have a number of conservative acquaintances (Some are actually very good friends, though ill-informed.) in the corporate world who have a problem with teachers and professors who have gained tenure in their positions. "Why should they have security in their jobs when we don't?" I wonder if they understand what kind of protection educators are being guaranteed? In what other field, besides elementary education, is a person with five years of college likely to have a starting salary of between $32,000 and $37,000 a year? When I lived in San Francisco, the street sweepers earned more than schoolteachers, who were responsible for helping to form the lives of our future generations. Why do the Japanese see this more clearly than we? Their teachers are elevated in status and compensated accordingly.

A problem that I have with education itself is that it seems to be involved in what sociologists call "cultural lag." When one aspect of culture is not keeping pace with another, the result is dissonant and dysfunctional for the culture. I don't think that education in our society has done a good job of assessing future needs and reacting accordingly. By the time we react, it is usually too late, and then new needs have emerged. Is it because we think organized education knows it all and it is incumbent upon the culture to take us through the time-consuming process of proving us wrong? Employers tend to be dissatisfied with the product we are sending them. I have good reason to believe them when they say that many not only cannot perform, but also cannot fill out the job application correctly. Where does the problem begin? Is it about incompetent teachers? Or does it go deeper? Is it about resources? About class size? About de-emphasizing reading, writing, and critical thinking? I am a witness to unbelievable teacher dedication, for my wife, Sue, works long hours at school each day and comes home and does school work most often until midnight. I am also aware of the dedication of my colleagues who go well beyond professional demands without proper compensation, even when economic times are good. Where are the parents in the primary and secondary school process? Isn't it supposed to be a collaborative effort between school and home? Lately, because of dual-income families, the job of making Little Johnny a human being has been handed off to the schools.

The same task-packed scenario applies to those who teach at the college level. I am very aware of my own workload and commitment as a college educator. But, again, my continual exposure to the work of my colleagues, especially English professors, has shown me that their burden is even heavier. I am certain that other disciplines exercise the appropriate diligence in their delivery of instruction. But what I have been exceptionally impressed with is the almost total attention given to meticulously assessing and grading papers, not only at term's end, but week in and week out. It is amazing to me that so many people perpetuate several poisonous myths about education and educators without bothering to check the facts. Many believe that teachers work only a half day, nine months each year, at inflated wages; that, because of the tenure system some institutions employ, teachers have the security of lifelong employment; and that "those who can, do and those who can't, teach." My survey of students in my classes indicates that there are talented people who would like to choose education as a career, but for the meager compensation. To be a successful and gratified teacher, one has to accept that the profession is a labor of love. If lucrative financial compensation is the goal, best to look elsewhere.

A major benefit that my chosen career has provided for me is exposure to the many worlds other than my own. In the fields of Anthropology and Sociology, the opportunity to interface with the variety of cultures in our midst is boundless. The students seem to think that they are being taught what I know. The truth is that, while I may present the potential for them to explore new directions for themselves, acting on that potential is their job. And in the process of our interplay, from the beginning of this wonderful, rewarding career, I have been absolutely convinced that I stand to learn more from those who sit with me than the other way around, for over the past thirty-nine years there have been far more of them than me. I have not only been exposed to the values and beliefs that come out of a wide variety of racial, religious, and ethnic homes, such as political inclinations, myths about racial superiority and sacred intolerance, but also have had the opportunity to help to dispel, with their assistance, unfounded ideas. The socialization process begins at home, and the classroom is where I pick up clues as what is being discussed and promoted in those homes. The notions that are established during those crucial first five years are almost etched in granite, unless dislodged by more dominant forces, such as intelligence born of critical thinking and positive personal experiences. Open, no holds-barred seminar discussions allow for such exchange of ideas, and I have witnessed massive growth and development occur over time with a number of students. This does not mean that when the dust settles everyone agrees. It means that now individuals can entertain the idea of new possibilities, even as they walk away convinced that they had been right in the first place.

26

THE NATURE
OF BUREAUCRACY . . .

As wonderful as the low-paying, high-gratification field of education may be, it does have, by its very nature, intrinsic problems. It is bureaucratic. For our own good mental health, it behooves us all to appreciate the inevitability and the positive consequences of bureaucracy even as we suffer its indignities. Conventional wisdom tells us that with all of its warts, bureaucracy is absolutely essential to the well-being of a society with the size and complexity of ours. Our aversion to bureaucracy includes the standard criticisms: red tape, hierarchy, impersonality, inefficiency, excessive paperwork, and unbending policy. Unfortunately, all of these characteristics are necessary for the smooth flow of information, products, and people. Bureaucracies are never as efficient as they could be. They tend to work up to minimum requirements. No more. No less. Workers are more likely to do what they are required to do, as specified in their job descriptions. Bureaucracies have to ensure that there are no obstacles to achieving the minimal standards, often at the expense of achieving excellence.

Red tape is necessary for consistent policy, which accounts for avoiding getting bogged down in having to hesitate to contemplate each individual element in the process. With few exceptions, we all prefer to be regarded as individuals, recognized for our uniqueness and appreciated for our positive contributions. Bureaucracy does not allow for that. If we understand that from the outset, we can survive it and maintain that good mental health. The second greatest betrayal that I have felt, second only to the experience with my earlier Sunday school teacher's disappointment, happened more recently in the bureaucratic setting at my college. Actually, this was a far more vicious and shocking betrayal than the first because it was aimed directly at me by a long-standing "acquaintance" (I almost said friend) who had managed to weave her way into my confidence as few others have. It happened when I felt the urge to apply for one of the deanship openings at my college, with pretty good confidence that I would be a viable candidate, since I had thirteen years of credible experience as a dean in our district, having developed most of the service programs from scratch and reestablished the integrity of one program that was being dragged through the mud every day in the local papers. I had used pretty good judgment in selecting what I thought were fine staff. (Most are still with us after twenty to twenty-five years.) But nothing in human dynamics is ever one hundred percent pure, and some very scary ones managed not only to sneak through, but also to squirm into the good graces of the powers that be. The most notorious of them all was a counselor that I brought in and who was forever singing my praises and referring students to me. I was the greatest thing ever. But I was still a slow learner. And a dear friend, Pat Conner, who was my secretary at one time (she now coordinates the Learning Center at Santa Ana College) warned me to be very careful about this one and to never turn my back on her, for she would do anything to promote her own interests. I did not believe it and saw no need for concern. I should have.

When I was a finalist for the dean's position and was told by the acting president that the "stars were not properly aligned," I filed a complaint with the Fair Employment and Housing Department to arrange for an investigation to find out exactly what had happened. I was asked by the agency if I knew anyone by this woman's name. "Well," they said, "she is not your friend. In her reference statement she indicated that you were unorganized." This from a woman who had always commented on how structured and organized my work had been. It occurred to me that there had to be some collusion involved, for, since I was not in competition with her in any way, she had no vested interest in my demise. I was not nearly as disappointed with not getting the job as I was with my loss of trust in humankind. As a matter of fact, I am likely to live a longer, healthier, and more satisfying life doing what I do. This was a woman whom a colleague and I have heard belittle and denigrate her own supervisors and peers with the disclaimer, "But don't say that I said it." My only personal recourse was to warn all who worked for and with her to "always watch your back." Unfortunately, when so-called "leaders" are revealed for their shortcomings, too often they get kicked upstairs. Good organizational skills, but short on interpersonal prowess except to smile a lot. It is the bureaucratic "Peter Principle" at work, which is likely to reveal itself in due time. As the old folks used to say, "God don't like ugly." Being a credentialed counselor myself, I tend to expect more sensitivity and integrity from anyone in the profession. But, there's that blind trust thing again.

I established earlier that I am unequivocally dedicated to gender equity. However, in a conversation with a female colleague I lamented the scurrilous betrayal mentioned above and my dedication to gender equity began to erode slightly–temporarily. For the first time I began to question if certain types of behaviors, such as back-stabbing or sneakiness or not being up-front, were more ascribable to females than males. I was assured that both genders are capable of being self-serving and that it happens fairly routinely in bureaucracies, regardless of gender. But I still wonder if all the new opportunities open to women make them play the game as they perceive men playing it. Do they assume that trickery and subterfuge are simply an integral part of bureaucratic culture? I have since learned that no indication to the contrary is likely to dampen my enthusiasm for gender equity. The impression made on me in my formative years was so profound that one less-than-scrupulous individual will not likely dislodge my commitment to what is fair, right, and decent.

27

POLITICS

Since politics, by definition, is competition for power, it follows that the concept is fraught with the potential for evil. But I have found it necessary to look for the silver lining, for there is always one to be found, and finding it makes it a lot easier to deal with the inevitable nastiness. In government, the legislative process has on occasion actually worked in remedying some concerns of the disenfranchised, typically, though, only after getting the attention of the power structure by "hitting it upside the head with a two-by-four," which is a sad commentary on our society. Such motivation should not be necessary. It engenders conflict for the long term. The society is reactive, too often, to negative stimuli only. Introductory political science teaches us that those who hold power never give it up willingly. What is worse, ours is a society with the capability to anticipate trouble coming down the pike, but which never makes adjustments until slapped across the face. If ignored long enough, it is thought, problems will go away. The truth is, they seldom do. In fact, they tend to grow in size and intensity.

The political institution in this country has never been pretty, nor is it likely to become so. Presently, I am having a personal crisis trying to figure out how the electorate in this country can be so apathetic and gullible. We are blessed with two major parties that bear serious scrutiny, maybe one a little more than the other. We are observing some promising changing dynamics on the political scene. Increasing numbers of both voters and politicians are daring to take a look at new possibilities with regards to philosophy and even affiliation. More and more are thinking outside of the box. Political parties will find it increasingly difficult to take any faction for granted. The proliferation of lobbyists and political action committees, which often have more influence over representatives than the constituents they should be serving, has brought into question the validity of the system.

My own political orientation is influenced by a lifetime of witnessing blatant injustice and a system which has been slow to redress debilitating social problems. It is clear that what progress has been made in the twentieth century has occurred on the Democrats' watch, for the most part. Being a product of the second half of the twentieth century, my perspective relates significantly to the series of social events of that period, probably beginning with World War II, but came into its own during the most active Civil Rights years, with all of its bitterness. The *blue skies* of that era were the raising of the consciousness and self-concept of African-Americans in this country. It brought a watershed of positive change, and things would never be the same again. None of this is to say that we've arrived and that we've reached that "promised land" of which Dr. King spoke. My perspective continues to be shaped by the lack of opportunities for inner city youth, where unemployment for young black males hovers around fifty percent. And my perspective is not improved with the rising rate of hate crimes, overrepresentation of the disenfranchised on the unemployment rolls, and the high number of them without health insurance.

Neither politics nor justice is blind, which accounts, in large part for the near absence of women and blacks in the top 350 corporations in this country. Or in the Fortune Five Hundred, for that matter. Make no mistake about it. This state of affairs is no accident. You'd think that a system as flawed as ours would have been asleep at the switch on occasion, permitting a couple of "undesirables" to sneak through. But it seems that the gatekeepers become alert at the mention of such possibilities. The pabulum that we are fed as rationale for the history of exclusionary practices is offensive to the sensibilities and tastes of any intelligent person, regardless of orientation. Not qualified? Indeed! Why is it that more than fifteen nations have had female prime ministers or presidents, but the United States, "on the leading edge of progress," has never, to date, managed to see fit to break the trend with regards to either blacks, other minorities or females. But that has the potential to change in the near future. What is just as important in choosing leaders is to not make the mistake of selecting individuals based solely on race, ethnicity, or gender. In fact, if Barack Obama is successful in his quest for the presidency, it is likely to be *in spite of* his race, and not *because of* that liability. Lately, there has been more and more talk about the likelihood that even some people who are convinced that he will best satisfy our needs, may succumb to race as an issue once behind the polling curtain. That is sad and ignorant in enlightened times. In the recent primary election, the female who was vying for the Democratic nomination, Hillary Clinton, though very well qualified, brought along enough baggage and some low trustworthiness and honesty ratings that many voters, including some women, were reticent to support her. Men, especially, had a problem with her, probably unjustifiably so. It is a liability to be strong and competent women in leadership roles. Also, there was the problem with Bill. Geraldine Ferraro encountered a husband's business problems as she ran for the Vice Presidency some years ago. In both cases there were cries of sexism. Was there? It is very much a matter of the character of those who rise to the position of challenger. In the past, it has been very clear that sexism was prevalent in our choices of leaders. And it still exists. Why, we've not even passed the Equal Rights Amendment, which was first introduced in 1923, giving women equal protection under the Constitution. What is amazing is that women voters outnumber their male counterparts by a significant margin. But they, like the rest of us, often do not vote in accordance with what they perceive to be best, overall, for themselves, such as the case in the last primary election. However, on occasion, the tendency has been to do what they perceive to be what is in the best interest of the country as a whole. Women have been willing to sort out what is good for the country, such as Senator McCain's ill-advised choice of Governor Sarah Palin as his running mate, a choice rejected by many women. The choice was another example of the "Peter Principle" at work. Ascending to the position of mayor of her small town was doable, which is often easily achieved because few others want the job. Then being elected as governor of the sparsely populated state of Alaska, probably due to name recognition, with a reputation for being vindictive, authoritarian, and abusive of the powers of the office. The "Peter Principle" is about rising to one's level of incompetency. This usually occurs in bureaucracies as the result of individuals accepting one promotion too many. They were just fine in their last position, but probably should have thought twice about accepting the new one.

The choice that is being made by women, according to the polls, seems to be more pragmatic, which is as it should be. The upshot of Hillary Clinton's loss in the primaries was massive disappointment on the part of her supporters—especially women who were seeing this as their chance, who then became disgruntled, feeling disenfranchised and consequently threatened to either vote for the opposition party or to not vote at all. Forget about principles. The epitome of short-sightedness. It is loyalty gone awry. As it turned out, they came to their senses after blowing off some pent-up steam.

At this writing, I'm going out on a limb and predict that, barring a major catastrophe, the Democrats, in the person of Barack Obama, will win the upcoming presidential election, given the nature of their opposition and their proposals for the economy. If race does become an issue, it will tell us volumes about this society. And if race really is a factor, it definitely will not be because of younger voters. They seldom carry the same racial baggage as their predecessors.

My rationale for making such a prediction has to do with our political system's tendency to correct itself by checks and balances with regards to political party dominance. When one party gets us into too much trouble, then, as gullible as the public is, it tosses them out and brings in the second shift. In the case of George W. Bush, we simply waited too long to correct our course. Both parties readily admit that the Republicans have done a horrible job with governance on a number of levels, including the war in

Iraq and the economy. Concerned citizens are also bothered about our loss of stature among other nations, including our friends. It will take years and extraordinary effort to regain the respect this country has enjoyed historically. Our problem, then, was exacerbated by the electorate foolishly giving George W. Bush a second term. The first term should have been enough for us to see what we were dealing with (Fool me once, it's your fault. Fool me twice, it's my fault). We should have benefited from hindsight. That is one of the important values of history. But it is not all about blaming either political party for the terrible fix we're in. The greed on Wall Street is a microcosm of the larger society. The larger society has a greed problem, too. When the Frenchman Alexis de Tocqueville who toured America in 1831 wrote in his book, *Democracy in America*, he noted that Americans are not ever quite satisfied with what they have. They always want more. We have a tendency to want more than we have earned. Thus, credit. Neither Wall Street nor Main Street has learned to adhere to the edict "Never spend more than what you have." We know what the inevitable consequences will be, but our addiction keeps pushing us deeper into the abyss.

Other minorities (and, yes, in spite of their superior numbers, women are minorities) are also disproportionately represented in oblivion. When the society witnesses a few high profile blacks, for example, the conclusion drawn is that "They're doing well," or "They've arrived." It is not uncommon for organizations to place minorities in executive positions, and then feel no obligation to diversify the rank and file. After all, "We've got one." And often the "One" that they've got is not sensitive to the needs of those left behind. It is a gigantic error for minorities to fall for that one. It is a mentality and practice that extends into professional entertainment and athletics, although those should be the least of our concerns. Minority faces and bodies filling the screens of movies and television do not mean that any of them stretch beyond what is very apparent to our sensibilities. The images that we perceive represent a minute fraction of all the "wannabees." It's the tip of the "wannabee" iceberg. And what have been the benefits to the rest of society, which could make very good use of some of the inflated salaries that often disappear in smoke or dust? We too often mistakenly see their successes as our own, and so we get lulled into complacency. When their fame dissipates, so do our hopes and dreams. The society's focus on sports and entertainment needs to be seriously reevaluated in terms of the resources we are willing to expend on them, as we increasingly neglect more important institutions, such as education and health care. Both of these institutions have more and more become political footballs and tend to take the first and largest hits in times of fiscal constraints. Talk of preemptive strikes! It is a very convenient way of keeping the disadvantaged where they are. As painful as it is, our attitudes toward education and health care are obviously a reflection of emerging societal values. That is, because these institutions have been traditionally inaccessible to those without power, there is no reason to change the order of things. I plead with my students to make it their business to re-examine some of our more serious thoughts as they impact their futures and the futures of their children and grandchildren. I am convinced that a few will actually become change agents.

28

RACE AND ETHNICITY

All aspects of my life have been impacted by race and ethnicity. I have, on occasion, been guilty of forgetting the nature of my environment and my place in it. I often wonder how that can be possible, having had the Birmingham experience in my most formative years. Trying to figure it out is a taxing and challenging task. I am not sure that I have solved the mystery. What I do know is that I feel grateful for not feeling permanently debilitated by those years. And I am not oblivious to the horrible things that still exist in this society. At the risk of seeming presumptuous or arrogant, I simply feel bigger than my adversaries. They have the problem. It is my job to see to it that their blemishes don't spill over into my life; therefore, I do keep half an eye open for the "uglies." They are always there. That means everywhere. They have not given up and are very busy at convincing us all that there is a revitalization movement afoot. And there is. If this seems like paranoia, simply take a look at the Internet information on hate groups, along with daily news accounts of discriminatory practices and deep-seated institutional policies that continually have to be challenged. Never mind that complainants would much rather expend their time and effort on more contention-free and pleasant endeavors.

It stands to reason that Anthropology has established that there is no place for race in anthropological equations, since any factor in the equations must be pure. Because there are no longer pure races, the discipline has concluded that, while race has sociological implications, it has no place in anthropology. Sociologically, race and racism are significant. Important decisions are often made about people based solely on race in this society, decisions that impact people's access to life-defining resources, e.g., employment, housing, education, and health care. It should be comforting to doubters that the special programs that were designed to alleviate some past disparities have been largely unsuccessful. Even in its heyday, affirmative action was subjected to several strategies to circumvent the rules, such as using tokens as window-dressing or using the old "But, you were a finalist" routine in the selection processes or simply ensuring that minorities are included in the pool of eligible candidates. But for them, there is the proverbial "Glass Ceiling," of which Arlie Hochschild of UC Berkeley speaks, relative to women's potential for progress. They can see beyond that ceiling, but they're not going to get there. I have wondered if anyone has figured out the fact that always being the bridesmaid doesn't cut it. In fact, debilitating psychological harm is often done by the rejection felt by "also-rans." Resistance to special, ameliorating programs has resulted from the mistaken belief that they were designed to favor the unqualified over the qualified. That was never the intent of the policies. The intent was to have open access for all. Violations of the policy did occur, of course, as uninformed decision makers misconstrued the intent, setting off a rash of anger that has not abated to this day. John McCain recently voted to ban it in Arizona. I'd like to assure him that he needn't worry. It doesn't work anyway.

Several years ago at Irvine Valley College in Orange County, California, I taught a course called Sociology of Racial and Ethnic Groups. The course dealt primarily with the several Asian, Latino, Native American, and African-American groups. I was struck by two things that are often overlooked by too many people. First, because of sheer laziness, we tend to categorize all Asian-Americans, Native Americans, and Latinos without consideration of individual ethnicities among each group. Japanese-Americans, Chinese-Americans, Korean-Americans, Filipinos, East Indians, and Southeast Asians are all thrown into the same cubby without regard for cultural differences. This is no less true of Latinos, who emanate from vastly different geographic origins with vastly different customs and values. The various origins are Mexico, Puerto Rico, Cuba, and Central and South America, all with distinct histories and backgrounds. It takes too much effort to pause long enough to figure out what makes each group tick. And so, we work from lists of stereotypes that can be terribly misleading and cause damaging error in judgment. Second, in preparing a lecture on a Sunday afternoon, I noticed that if I would draw a line through the mention of any of the racial or ethnic groups and insert "women," the same inequities ascribed to the racial and ethnic groups would apply to women. It is that lack of power and influence that makes women a minority group right along with racial and ethnic minorities, since minority status is based on relative power—not relative numbers. I have noticed that some women have been deluded into believing that they are on equal footing with white males. Others have been simply co-opted and joined the ranks of middle-management go-fers, who are necessary cogs nonetheless. I know. I was one of them.

Ethnicity issues do not stop with people of color. We have not paid an awful lot of attention to white ethnicity until there were reports of "ethnic cleansing" in Bosnia. How could there be an ethnic problem there when there are no blacks or browns or yellows? White ethnicity is significant in this country. A brief look at white enclaves in the Midwest and New England is a convincing reminder of the importance of the differences people make among themselves. Neighborhoods are often self-contained and exclusionary. Outsiders are regarded as the threatening enemy and, so, are not welcomed. Ethnicity is about cultural differences and the extent to which groups will go to establish and maintain those differences. Few in our society are aware that the largest white ethnic group among us is German-Americans. Many believe the group to be Irish-Americans, who are actually a distant second to the German-Americans.

We have the tendency to think in terms of black and white when we think of group differences. But there really are other groups that make up this country, and the feelings of antipathy are almost as strong among them as towards those who have different physical appearances. And reference is always made to one's ethnicity, even when it has no bearing whatsoever on the subject at hand. I've noticed that in part of New England, even the dead are interned in segregated cemeteries so that they may rest assured that they will not be contaminated by the "others," even in death. These communities are microcosms of population deployment throughout the world and account for the asininity of nations' inability to coexist peacefully.

I struggle to find the source of my attitude towards race and ethnicity. Especially race. Ethnicity as a concept did not occur to me until late adolescence and early adulthood, resulting from the Italian and Jewish businesses in my childhood communities and later from my exposure to incredible diversity in the Marines. The childhood experiences simply informed me that there were groups among us that were different. The Marine Corps taught me that, yes, there are different groups in the mix, but that none are superior or inferior to any other. I harken, again, back to a profound statement that Leo Buscaglia made when he referred to what he called "the Democratic Character…That there is no one any better or worse than we are," a thought African-Americans and Latinos should keep in mind as they go about beating up on each other. There are those with power and influence who are quite contented to watch Blacks and Browns body-punch each other to death. We're all in the same boat, as far as the majority is concerned. Those in the same boat would be wise to paddle together. When I examine my own orientation, I am always reminded of Buscaglia's statement mentioned above regarding the "Democratic Character." That orientation is especially significant in light of my early beginnings in Birmingham. But perhaps it was that very grounding in African-American communities in Birmingham, especially Mama and the high schools, which set me up to feel worthy and to resist anything or anyone that would challenge that self-concept: the phenomenal Mrs. Lucille Boyd (most memorable teacher), Mr. George Bell (junior high school principal), Mr. R. C. Johnson (Parker High School principal), and Cleve from Walt's Shell Station (folk wisdom without peer).

I once attempted to deny that I had been scarred by racism, going about my life in normal fashion. But that was at a more naïve stage of my development. I saw most things as they should be, not as they are. It is said that ignorance is bliss (again, if it doesn't harm you), and I suppose there is some benefit to being oblivious to the dangers all around us. And so, psychosis and paranoia were not issues to be dealt with until the sting of brutal reality found its mark. I wondered if the source of my unsuspecting nature was Mama's over-protectiveness in my early years. The *blue skies* are that I have tended to not be obsessed with suspicion, which I personally feel is counter-productive and debilitating. It is closely akin to the "Doubtful Dora" stories that Mrs. Boyd used to tell us in the fifth and sixth grades at Cameron School. It is funny how those messages continue to be relevant regardless of the glut of changes that have occurred over the five or six decades. Unfortunately, we often find ourselves necessarily having to fall either in the category of "skeptic" or of "naïve optimist," both of which can be dangerous. Somewhere along the line I began to feel more comfortable looking at the brighter side of things, letting the chips fall where they may. For the most part, for my own good mental health, things have worked out, even though on some occasions I have emerged with a bloody nose. But bloody noses eventually stop bleeding.

I find it necessary to think in terms of the devastating effects of what racism has done to entire groups of people, rather than its ill effects on individuals, myself included. More than the psychological effects are the social effects, including exclusion in the economic sphere and the generational consequences that necessarily follow. Anyone who claims not to recognize the consequences chooses not to recognize them, for they are plainly visible to anyone with an iota of intelligence. The naysayers are beginning to have a few problems these days because the disenfranchised are more and more including people who look like themselves. And then what do you do? Do you dismantle the systems that are supposed to serve as safety-nets for those who are hurting? And just who are those people? Take a close look at the representation by race of people on welfare. While getting over that shock, take a further look at welfare fraud by race, by state. These data are readily available on the Internet. In both instances, Whites swell those rolls.

The really frightening thing about racism is that racists, like others practicing other "isms," believe they are functioning from a position of righteousness. Nations fight wars with fervor because they feel that theirs is a just cause. Some religions denigrate others because the others are heathens who are destined to burn in hell. Men practice sexism because they are convinced that it is written that they are superior to women. And all that is necessary to prevail is to seriously believe that you are in a righteous position. As Joe Louis, the then heavyweight champion of the world, proclaimed on billboards in World War II, "We know we're gonna win, because we're on God's side." Absurd. Surely, Hitler believed he was right in expunging six million Jews and programming for Aryan racial superiority. "Isms" are often difficult to counter because their believers are not bound by empirical fact. There is never a payoff in a debate where rationality and critical thinking doesn't count. It will be really interesting to see how all of this dogma plays out in face of globalization, which makes the world a smaller, more connected and interdependent place. Will we necessarily have to figure a strategy to co-exist peacefully, or as the saying goes, "Live together or die together"?

29

AND THEN THERE
ARE THE OLD
FOLKS . . .

An "ism" that is not given nearly enough thought in our society today is "ageism." As a society, we are getting older with each passing generation. I am amazed that this country, with all of its resources, has not come up with a plan to deal with this phenomenon. "Older Americans" of today are not the "older Americans" of a short time ago. They are physically, socially, and economically more vital. They value their independence. Physical acuity impacts mental acuity, and older people enjoy more of both in today's society. For society, this means that younger segments of the population will need to think in terms of moving over to make room for folks who will not be denied. This means increased vitality for the society as there are more people to make meaningful contributions to its good health. There are more elderly people in our society than teenagers.

When I ask if they have had courses in gerontology, students most often give a blank, open-mouth stare. They have no idea whatsoever to what I am referring. At the very root of the problem is the total misconception of what the aging process is all about. This is due, in large part, to our society's emphasis on youth and contempt for anyone over forty. It is no wonder that so many of us "freak out" as we are about to cross that line into "inconsequentiality." But just wait. They'll get theirs. There was actually a time in my Anthropology, Sociology, and Marriage and Family classes when I pretty much glossed over chapters involving aging and the elderly, justifiably so, I thought, because I could sense that young students simply zoned out at the mention of something so depressing. On one occasion, we were discussing the stereotypes that young people have about older people when the issue of sexuality arose. Some were genuinely hard put to imagine their own parents having sex—especially with each other. One young woman in the back of the room, with a painful expression on her face, exclaimed, "Yuk! Sloppy sex!"

The stereotypes abound. "Old people talk too much." I tell them that maybe if the elderly received more attention from young people, they might not be so desperate for interaction. When I read meters for the Gas Company, I would often get trapped in the homes of old women who offered coffee and cookies and who had volumes of information to share. It was obvious that they were starving for company and though meter readers tend to be people in a hurry, I found it difficult to pull myself away and get on with running and jumping over hedges and fences to beat my allotted route time.

"Old people are whiners and are too dependent." Quite the contrary. We older people don't want anything from the young, especially our children.

The greatest gift we'd like from you is for you to be self-sufficient and independent. That signifies to us that we have done our job. We want you up and running and out of the house. Forget that mush about the "empty-nest syndrome." And we don't want you out just for an increase in our personal space, or so that we can run around the house nude. In fact, we'd love to have you visit us on occasion. But what is so important to us is for you to prove your readiness to survive in our absence.

"Yeah, but old people are stingy." I get this often from young people who have worked as servers in restaurants and don't feel that they have been adequately rewarded with gratuities for their less-than-adequate service. I tell them to try growing up in The Depression years and even beyond. And try living on a fixed income. And try to imagine the fear of outlasting your money. My personal tendency is to over-tip for exceptional service. But they'd better get it while the getting is good, for things are likely to tighten up a bit as time passes.

"And old people stink." Usually, it's more about overindulgence in perfume for older women or the aroma of Ben-Gay rather than inattention to personal hygiene for men, though sometimes the memory processes may fade, and personal hygiene may become secondary to naps. And, yes, sometimes old men forget to unzip their flies before relieving themselves. Older women may be forgiven for losing some of their olfactory senses and wind up dousing themselves with perfumes. Better safe than sorry? Most of us can remember being almost suffocated by those too-sweet gases in church or at weddings or funerals. Lately, it has been at plays or concerts where the air becomes sickening. Young people complain that old people's houses are "musty" and rancid. Old stuff is likely to have old odors. It's important to be reminded that the "old stuff" is likely to be the treasures of time gone by and, therefore, highly valued by their owners.

"Old people are grumpy and set in their ways." Grumpy could be a result of something hurting or disillusionment with new-fangled ideas. Often we are too comfortable with the familiar. Don't confuse us with the facts. We trust what has gotten us this far and are often suspicious of change. This is probably one of our biggest mistakes. Change is inevitable and is ever accelerating. And this is not about change simply for the sake of change. Any dynamic society will entertain the notion of change in response to emerging needs and attitudes. Much of our resistance is a result of fear of the unknown. But intergenerational conflict is not a problem exclusive to old people. Both groups, the young and the old, feel that they possess all of the answers, and neither does. If only they would listen to each other. They would likely learn that there is time-tested relevance in all that we know, understanding that technological advances and changing social values will dictate that all of us make some adjustment to our point of view. It is a monumental error for the young to discard the massive accumulation of knowledge gathered over generations. It is true that much of that information is outmoded, but a goodly amount of it may prove to be increasingly valuable as time passes. We should be very careful about what we throw away. "You don't throw the baby out with the bath water."

A major criticism of old people is "They can't drive." As much as I'd like to defend us on that score, I am afraid that I can't do so in good conscience. Some of us need to recognize when it is time to give it up. When we are getting too many "honks" from people, both drivers and pedestrians, whom we have come close to decapitating, we should at least wonder "What just went wrong?" I live in a city in close proximity to a "senior city." It is a very large complex with several gates around its perimeter. It can be a hazardous experience if you find it necessary to be in the vicinity when some of the residents exit with excessive aplomb and seem to be in a world of their own. I have witnessed, on more than one occasion, people exiting a gate, proceeding to the far left lane and then making a right turn at the intersection. If you then look in amazement at what they just did, they give you a stare of indignation, that is, if they are aware of your presence at all. Many simply see a strong connection between aging and entitlement. You might also be amazed at a vehicle that appears to have no driver at all. There is no head visible, and the only evidence of humanity in the car is two sets of white knuckles squeezing the steering wheel. I make it a point to stay out of the vicinity of retirement communities when possible, to maintain my distance when I have no choice, and to assume that something spectacular is likely to happen, at any moment, either ahead of me or behind me. And I am an old person.

I am not one who believes that life happens in non-negotiable increments. If we are individually different, then it stands to reason that our interests and capabilities can also be vastly different. We should not necessarily shift into a new mode simply because it is the next day and it is our birthday. We certainly shouldn't delude ourselves into believing that we are still teenie-boppers and act accordingly. We should be smart enough to recognize when true transitions are occurring. And we will be amply notified with increased aches and pains, with gravity taking hold and, most importantly, with a decrease in mental prowess. The key is to avoid denial, which only serves to fool ourselves. It's like the mismatched, poorly fitted toupee. The only one who thinks that it is undetectable is the wearer.

30

Marriage and Family

At the end of my journey, I will have left an indelible mark on world population. Even as I encourage my students to produce only one-and-a-half children per family, I have fathered eight, at a time when such insanity was pretty normal. But I love all eight children, all nineteen grandchildren (one pending), and all six great grandchildren. A major part of this configuration was definitely not planned parenthood.

Because fifty-five years of my life has been spent as a married person and because of the peaks and valleys (maybe I should say valleys and peaks), I have accumulated a healthy portfolio on the nature of relationships. Some of the data are based upon personal perspective, but some are more universal and pervasive, e.g., teaching Marriage and Family courses for a number of years and garnering new insights from students as we moved along. I am encouraged, in spite of my contemporaries' opinion to the contrary, that many of the younger ones have healthier ideas of what it takes to make good relationships than some of the elderly. Many older people like to put the young down, accusing them of not having the "wonderful" principles that they, themselves, had. Some of those principles are what got us into so much trouble, such as choosing to marry because it was what society expected of us. What the young ones have learned is that it is not society that has to deal with the agony year on end.

And then there was sex. How many males and females got married just for sexual access or because of inadvertent pregnancy? Of course, an answer to the problem is abstinence and avoiding inadvertent pregnancies. But who are the "Just say no" people fooling? The hope is that as young people look to their futures, they will understand the need to exercise caution and behave more responsibly. *It takes only a split second to obliterate a future.* I feel unbelievably fortunate to have survived the biggest mistake of my life. Mine is not the best example for young people to follow, except that if mistakes are made, they do not necessarily spell doom. Who among us has not made mistakes? The key here is not to be subdued by them and, for young folks, to realize that there is actuarially more life ahead than behind them. The two males that I had shared dreams of the future with the most as a child, as we contemplated families, lifestyles, etc., were my best friend, William and my cousin, Harold. For some reason, I wondered if either of them managed to correct the course of their lives and extricate themselves from less than desirable domesticate situations—to the very end when their wives were deceased. In that regard, I was probably the fortunate one for being able to pull out, with the help of unknown forces.

The *blue skies* are not always that easy to recognize. As the physical maladies visit upon us more and more frequently and increasingly in new places, aging people forget the carefree times when all systems, physical and mental, were generally intact. More and more it seems that our conversations with peers revolve around nothing but our health problems. It is not unusual for us to forget what we called on the phone about in the first place. It turns out to be commiseration with bad news one-up-manship. On reflection, though, we might recall that there have probably been worse pitfalls in our lives that we overcame, and if not, now is a new adventure, for which we will need to gear up in order to survive. When we stop to think of what a wonderful machine the human body is, of its ability to regenerate itself, and of its inevitable decline, we should also stop and remember that patience is a supreme virtue, for, as Tolstoy claims in *War and Peace*, the strongest of all warriors are time and patience.

Far too often, skeptics have pronounced the family institution as either terminally ill or dead. The problem, many believe, began with the terrible forties, fifties, and especially the sixties. The sexual revolution, massive changes in gender roles, and the mass media have exposed us to too many things about which some people feel we should be kept ignorant. Among societies, we were categorized as an "a-sexual" culture, being devoid of sexuality. And while we define ourselves as such, our behavior has consistently belied the definition. But the family is not dead. It has simply gone through metamorphosis in response to changing social needs. Those of us who have been around for awhile tend to feel a bit uneasy about the vanishing traditional form and function of family, often forgetting the traditional dysfunctions that have made life miserable for many. Nothing evolves culturally unless those who are to be affected by the change want it and perceive a need for it. Many potentially great ideas have never come to fruition because they did not mesh well with the status quo or with the people's desires. Changes in our perception of family have come about because of changes in other aspects of the society. Nothing societal functions in a vacuum.

The fastest growing family type in our society is the single parent arrangement headed by a woman. Scores of adjustments have necessarily been made to conform to the new order of things. The new order of things has meant more women in the workplace (at about 25% less pay than males), more women playing dual gender roles, and more poverty among women and their children because of women's lesser earning capacity and the failure of fathers to meet their responsibilities for child support and/or spousal support. The *blue skies* are that there has been a lessening in stigma attached to being women and children in single-parent families. Conversely, the fastest decreasing family form is the nuclear family, composed of a mother, father, and their children, a major source of consternation for especially many old-timers who are stuck in time-warp. And as frightening as the new configuration may seem to us, it is simply a different approach to dealing with societal needs. As we look to the past, we notice that change in family form is not new to us. The intact family prior to the industrial revolution gave way to a disjointed, widely dispersed one that has become even more so as we move into the twenty-first century. Alienation has become commonplace among us to the point that interpersonal interaction has become increasingly difficult. Rather than viewing the changes as threatening, we should see them as naturally occurring phenomena gearing up to new needs.

Some people are concerned with the new level of legitimacy that alternate family forms are enjoying in a world where the thought is that eroding morals are at an all-time high. They are concerned about the lack of stigma attached to divorce, about single-parent households, about the melding of gender roles, about both parents working outside of the home, and about same-sex marriages, a major debate on the ballot in California at this time. On the surface, each of these situations could be problematic, for they bring about unprepared-for change from the traditional, familiar way of viewing the family. Upon taking a closer look, though, we find some of these changes are very practical and necessary. The society cannot tolerate a situation in which more than half of its people are disenfranchised. So, rather than ostracize those who, for whatever reason, find themselves among the divorced, the culture must make accommodations for such a massive proportion of its population. Downgrading the stigma is a significant move in that direction.

Single-parent households are not new to us. They are a logical consequence of the increased divorce rate, among other factors. In the past, these might have been families that would have remained intact due to social pressure to do so. The problem in the minds of many is exacerbated by the introduction of no-fault divorce, which some are convinced invites too many couples to go their separate ways without giving the relationship a fair chance to succeed. Some serious consideration should be given those who benefit from divorce by escaping untenable physical, psychological, sexual or verbal abuse. And the victims are far more likely to be women with little or no recourse. For economic reasons, Mama had no option but to remain in a horrible situation. Women really did often marry for a living. Fortunately, survival does not require that kind of torture today.

The melding of gender roles is a natural outcome of the events in history that put women alongside men in the workplace. This led to the sharing of responsibilities in the office, in the shop, and in the home. The last sixty years have given us change unimagined for most of the first half of the twentieth century, mostly due to enlightenment and necessity. As we move lithely into the twenty-first century, we can expect even more of this sharing, especially in domestic affairs including child-rearing, household chores and decision-making. This bodes well for a kinder and gentler society.

In spite of the common belief that the dual-earner family is absolutely necessary for a family to survive in today's economy, I plead with those who have not gone into the family-making business yet to avoid falling for the party-line and give the single income approach a chance first. Of course, in some instances two incomes are necessary simply to put food on the table and a roof overhead. Obviously, these basic needs must be satisfied before most other considerations. We do what we have to do. In many cases, two incomes are not necessary for survival, though they may seem to be so. But oftentimes people confuse survival with luxury. The payoff with single incomes in nuclear families is immeasurable. The benefits of children having a parent in the home during the day accrue to enormous proportions. Many avoidable problems arise after school hours when there is no monitoring of children's behavior, sometimes group behavior of a sexual nature. The rise in teen pregnancy can be partially attributed to such opportunities, especially for young teens. Some gruesome statistics can be found in some teen shelters in relatively affluent cities in my county where it is known that girls as young as eleven years old have reported being pregnant. The sooner the population realizes that curiosity about sexuality is not new to children and that social class and race and ethnicity do not provide exceptions, the better prepared it will be to meet the challenge. Ultimately, it is a matter of how that curiosity is dealt with by parents. Some parents have let their quest for the "little extras" that they might provide for their children get in the way of responsible parenthood. The "extras" tend to become worthless over time. It is the connections and relationships that withstand the test of time. I cannot count the number of young people I've heard declare in Marriage and Family classes that it is not the costly "things" that their parents provide for them (and there are many in this community of affluence) that matter. "What I would really like to have are my parents, to share my failures as well as my triumphs," they exclaim. "Too often," they say, "they are nowhere to be seen."

In spite of my own childhood background, this is a concept that caught on with me early on in my parenting experience. At the very top of my list of priorities has been and always will be my children. And if anyone wants to get on my bad side, a quick way to do it is to mess with them, with whatever flaws they may have. Along the way, some people have made the mistake of crossing that line and have probably wondered what hit them and what happened to my attitude towards them. I am quite aware that a large part of my defensiveness of my children today is a direct result of the horrible losses I endured beginning some decades ago.

The last of the eight children I fathered through two marriages are twins who are now approaching their thirty-third birthday. When the twins were born, epiphany of epiphanies! I figured out the cause of what seemed to happen about every three years since 1949. Why, this could go on forever if drastic measures were not taken. Drastic measures were taken. On my part.

With the births of Tia and Josh, my wife and I sat down to discuss the importance to both of us that someone remained home with them in their formative years. The plan was for five or so years. It extended to eight or nine. This obviously meant some economic sacrifice for a couple who was already living on the economic edge, both having nearly entry-level jobs, coupled with my responsibility for child support for five children. The *blue skies* were that we had a thorough understanding about our commitment to those responsibilities. For those first eight years all resources were pooled and used as needed without considering the sources. Now we discussed who would earn the paycheck and who would stay home with the twins and our six-year old, Semara. We agreed that I would continue to work as a relatively new college instructor and my wife, Sue, would be the homemaker. Somehow we pulled this off for about eight years without giving up anything of substance. In fact, I am convinced that we gained far more than we lost, for the only things lost were the "little extras," which quickly depreciate in value. What we gained was family. Semara always came home to an occupied abode. We had scheduled meals together. There seemed to be far less stress in the home, and there was more appreciation for the few "things" that we had than for the accumulation of the new "things" that we are now seem to be obsessed with protecting. A favorite recollection from the early years in our marriage is of a two-tiered bookcase constructed by assembling cement blocks and one-by-twelve boards. The memory of that bookcase will outlast any such furniture piece since. Sometimes our priorities become misaligned in the name of "progress."

This kind of insight may not occur to most of us until the latter part of our lives. Earlier on we may be too preoccupied with day-to-day survival, which may not leave much time for reflection on what really matters over the long term. Day-to-day survival often means working, planning the use of meager resources, and monitoring the upbringing of children. It seems that the opportunity to take stock of where we are in our lives and what it is all about doesn't present itself until we have pretty much conquered basic needs. Surplus and discretionary resources don't usually happen to us until we are too old to really enjoy them. So, we use them to spoil our grandchildren.

We get one meaningful shot at influencing the lives of our children, most often in the formative years. To the extent that we can continue to hold their attention beyond that, we may still have some impact. Leo Buscaglia speaks of the importance of the modeling role for parents, saying, "You be what you want your children to be and watch them grow."

As I look back, I am satisfied that I have come close to setting the tone for my children who would dare to listen and pay close attention. We, as parents, would hope to be the primary influences in children's lives, but it is important to remind ourselves that there are other, sometimes more powerful, forces out there, against which we are powerless. My divorce taught me that. I learned about the power of custodial parenting (which is why I sued for custody on three occasions). Those children who were estranged from me suffered the worse fates. Conversely, those who stayed closer to me, physically or emotionally, increased their opportunity for normalcy.

If there is one thing that is common among my children who have children of their own, it is the intense dedication they have for them. I absolutely love that. I have been criticized by a couple of colleagues for being overly supportive of my children and their children and their children. We don't do everything together, but many of our activities are, indeed, shared. When we dine out, it's reservations for fourteen. When we head for the mountains for a few days, it's a cabin for fourteen. When we do frequent trips to Maui, it's reservations for fourteen. It warms the heart to feel that young folks are willing to hang out with old fogies for extended periods of time.

Perhaps the greatest antidote to feelings of depression and hopelessness is to balance the positives in our lives with the inevitable negatives. On balance, the positives are likely to far outweigh the negatives. The bad things tend to stand out more prominently because in our rush to feel sorry for ourselves, we tend to forget the many high points. The mere fact that we are capable of waking each morning in relatively good health launches us into the day on the positive side. I have a good tennis acquaintance, Harvey Grimshaw, who likes to remind me and our fellow tennis players, "If you wake up in the morning and have no tag tied to your big toe, it's a good day." And, "If you begin the day looking down at the grass, as opposed to up at it, it's a good day." It seems to me that it is about what you do with the rest of the day. Wallowing in self-pity does nothing to solve problems; rather, it serves only to amplify them.

Problems are relative. If I seem a bit calloused and unsympathetic about other people's issues, perhaps it is because, though we are made of different kinds of stuff, we should all be able to deal with the routine curves that life tosses our way. Few people have had to recover from the loss of four children, as I have. We are all endowed with varying levels of resiliency, each with his or her own capacity to endure. We should be quick to reach for those reserves, however large or small they may be.

During the annual June gloom days in Southern California, when it might be depressingly overcast from morning to night, we find ourselves clamoring for just a glimpse of momentary relief in the form of sunshine. No matter how dreary, relief may be found as flights from Orange County Airport soar above the clouds to be greeted by bright sunshine and pure *blue skies*. They are always there. *There are always blue skies*. It is up to us to seek them out.

An Informed Afterword

It is now November 4, 2008 (Election Day) and Barack Obama has just won the election to become the forty-fourth president of the United States, obviously the first African-American to achieve this feat. The event has been called momentous, historical, emotional, and unbelievable. And it is all of those things. But in the context of what is fair, right, and decent, it is an event that is long overdue. Two compelling questions excite our curiosity: (1) what took it so long? and (2) what impact is it likely to have on race relations in this country as well as our image abroad?

Our history is very well known globally, including slavery, reconstruction, the vitriolic dynamics of the civil rights struggle, extreme ethnocentrism, and the after-taste resulting from painful relationships among groups within and without this society. So, it is not so difficult to understand why it took so long. We are still feeling some of the residual effects of those times. However, the jury is still out on the level of impact president-elect Obama's election will have on how we are perceived by world societies. Initial reactions appear to be very positive, which should not be surprising, given the contrasting negative image our culture has projected in international affairs over generations, especially over the past eight years.

It is also interesting to observe how Obama pulled this accomplishment off. It would be expected that considerable amount of support would come from African-Americans. And after Hillary Clinton was out of the picture in the primaries, two-thirds of Latinos came aboard as well. But most surprising was the turnout of young voters. I have given my young adult students all kinds of grief for abdicating their civic responsibilities by talking a good game but not showing up at the polls. In other words, walk the walk. They absolutely fooled me nationwide this time and were largely responsible for this phenomenal outcome. Will they keep it up? Or was this a unique call to arms? In spite of the doubts of some of my acquaintances, I am convinced that, even with residual problems, race relations and youth issues in this country will never be quite the same. For one very important thing, anyone who is disenfranchised by race, ethnicity, age, gender, social class, or disability will see new horizons and aspire to greater heights. And that is a tremendous gift to all children. Buscaglia notes that we have never found a limit to human potential. The hope is that this momentous occasion will be an eye-opener for future generations of all shapes and colors.

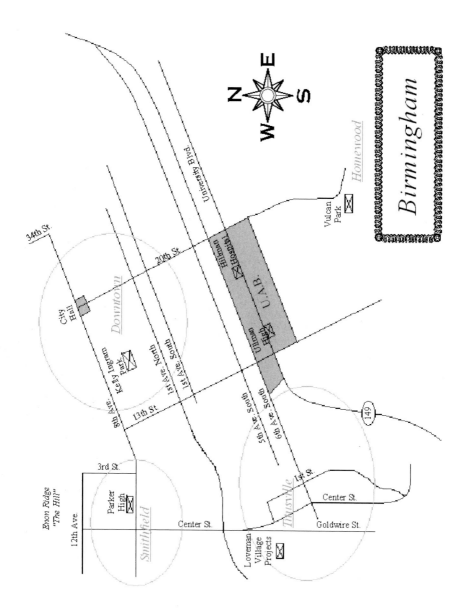

INDEX